*Praise for*
## THE SECRET TO HEALTH AND HAPPINESS

What a valuable tool Judy Ransom makes available to us. This practice of gratitude journaling has developed into a healthy daily habit for me. My day is not as anchored if I don't get my perspective grounded by doing this first thing in the morning.

I like to read back through my journal to look at evidence of God answering prayers. I especially like the gratitude prompts. I found I was getting a little stale and was always thanking God for the same things!

Judy provides scripture, devotions, and gratitude prompts that help keep me above my circumstances and ready to face whatever the day brings.

—CAROL MCCRACKEN,
Discipleship Minister

I would recommend this book to everyone I know. Every time I open it and begin to read, I am overwhelmed with a sense of peace. The Holy Spirit speaks to my heart and calms my anxious thoughts almost immediately.

Gratitude journaling has made a significant impact on my life. When my mind starts to fill up with negative thoughts toward someone who has hurt my feelings or mistreated me, I make a conscious choice to turn my mind toward thankfulness. I start thanking God for all of the good qualities in this person. It gives me greater perspective that this incident that upset me is not forever. It will pass.

The devotions are very relatable. Almost anyone has someone in their life with whom they have a complicated relationship. It has taught me that we can thank our way to peace in relationships. It has also helped me see that even though I am finding things to be thankful for, I must set firm boundaries with certain people.

When I am faithful to spend time in thankful meditation, I notice huge changes in my attitude. I am less stressed out, and I notice that I can put my circumstances in a better perspective. Even difficult things are more manageable.

I can't help but feel closer to God when I express thankfulness. He melts my heart through the wonderful reminders of how much He has given me. It humbles me so much when I consider all the gifts in my life that came only by His hand. I feel so loved by my heavenly Father!

Seeing what the author has gone through in her life and how God has transformed her heart and family relationships is evidence of how a thankful heart can transform your life.

—PATTI SMITH,
Publisher of *GO! Christian Magazine*

After a hurricane unexpectedly struck my area, I wrote in the gratitude journal *The Secret to Health and Happiness* every morning. This journal helped me stop focusing on my losses and look at what was spared. It turned my "poor me" attitude into a "blessed me" perspective.

—SUSAN U. NEAL RN, MBA, MHS
Best-selling author of *7 Steps to Get Off Sugar and Carbohydrates*

*The Secret to Health and Happiness* has been very beneficial for me. It helped me start and maintain a habit of recalling and recording all that I am thankful for on a regular basis.

I knew there were many benefits to being thankful, but to realize the effects of writing down these blessings has been a great help, especially first thing in the morning. Before my thoughts get caught away with distractions, this journal helps me focus on my blessings and start my day with a positive perspective.

I like the way *The Secret to Health and Happiness* is formatted in that there is plenty of space to write. I also enjoy being able to reference so many inspirational scriptures and quotes and reading the insightful devotions that all relate to thankfulness.

I recommend this to anyone who desires to start a life-changing habit that is very simple yet very profound.

—REV. DAVE DURIS,
Case Manager

I appreciate and love *The Secret to Health and Happiness* and have recommended it to family and friends. I am purchasing it for family gifts.

I read and write in it each day, and it is a daily reminder of how thankful I am for so many things we sometimes take for granted.

We always face challenges and difficulties in life. As believers, we are concerned about our country and our Christian values under attack. I read my Bible, pray, and endure, but am sometimes guilty of complaining. However, being thankful and having this book to journal gives me reminders and strength to carry on and know that God reigns. It changes my attitude and inspires me to love and serve God each day, thankful to Him.

—MARGARET TIDMORE,
Mentor Program Coordinator

To write things down is to clarify thoughts, which is why this gratitude journal is so effective. My life has been greatly impacted by realizing how much I'm thankful to God for and recognizing all the things that I have been taking for granted.

This kind of journaling gives the reward of a positive attitude. It keeps my thoughts "on a roll" in a positive direction.

This journal has "thankful" scriptures from the entire Bible, which blows my mind, because I wasn't aware there were that many. A true blessing to read them before writing.

Interspersed between journal sections are impactful Bible devotions, all with the "thankful theme." The author sheds light on several Bible accounts and passages. They are a joy to read!

I would recommend this book to anyone, both family and friends, because their lives would be enhanced by realizing how many things there are to be thankful for.

—SUE DURIS,
Substitute Teacher

Gratitude journaling has changed my life. At first, I thought there were too many lines to fill. But as I got into the book, I found myself searching my heart for additional things I am grateful for. I find myself digging into my past, remembering things that have brought me joy. So the additional lines are perfect. The devotions help inspire deeper gratitude.

It will be so much fun recommending *The Secret to Health and Happiness* to my family, friends, and clients. I know what some people are getting for Christmas.

—SUZANNE CARNILL,
Licensed Massage Therapist

# The SECRET to HEALTH and HAPPINESS

*Gratitude Journal*

*and Devotions*

John,

May grace and joy abound
to you through Thanksgiving!

Blessings,

*Judy Ransom*

## JUDY RANSOM

Editor: Janis Whipple
Cover Design: Angie Alaya
Interior Design: KUHN Design Group

*Dedicated
in gratitude
to Steve,
my soul mate and best friend.*

# CONTENTS

Acknowledgments . . . . . . . . . . . . . . . . . . . . . . . . . . . . . . . 11

Introduction . . . . . . . . . . . . . . . . . . . . . . . . . . . . . . . . . . 13

How to Use Your Gratitude Journal . . . . . . . . . . . . . . . . . . 17

1. Ten Lepers Healed—One Made Whole . . . . . . . . . . . . . . 27

2. Joy in His Presence—Giving Thanks . . . . . . . . . . . . . . . . 49

3. Forget Not All His Benefits—Or They'll Slip Away . . . . . . 71

4. The Fruit of Thankfulness—Taste and See . . . . . . . . . . . . 93

5. A Victor—Not a Victim . . . . . . . . . . . . . . . . . . . . . . . 115

6. Give Thanks—Not Complaints . . . . . . . . . . . . . . . . . . 137

7. In Everything Give Thanks—Through Good and Bad . . . . 159

8. Thankful for One Another—Even When It Isn't Easy . . . . 181

9. Thankful or Entitled? You Can't Be Both . . . . . . . . . . . . 203

10. The Forgiving Way to Gratitude—Not Easy, but Rewarding . . . 225

11. Gratitude Positioning System—The GPS That Always Works . . . 247

12. I Didn't Know What I Had—Till It Was Gone . . . . . . . . 269

Appendix A: Gratitude Prompts . . . . . . . . . . . . . . . . . 291

Appendix B: The Science of Gratitude . . . . . . . . . . . . . . 299

Notes . . . . . . . . . . . . . . . . . . . . . . . . . . . . . . . . . . . . . 303

About the Author . . . . . . . . . . . . . . . . . . . . . . . . . . . . 305

# ACKNOWLEDGMENTS

A writer's life can be isolated, occasionally venturing out of one's writing cave—in my case, the front bedroom office—to forage for food and water. These kitchen raids sometimes collide with those of my husband, Steve, as he seeks a reprieve from his forced isolation evoked by the cave dweller.

For his words of encouragement, despite his longsuffering sacrifice, I am humbled, thankful, and driven to love him more deeply than I ever thought possible.

Alas, the writer may wallow in the mere contentment of writing. It takes friends like Margaret Tidmore, who continually pester, "When are you going to publish this so I can give it to my family and friends?" to finally push the writer over the edge into the world of publication.

Susan Neal has taken my fledgling hand along a road she has oft traveled, leading me through each step of the publishing process. She also introduced me to the Word Weavers Destin writers' critique group. Each member's encouragement and critiques appear throughout this book.

Editors take the work of bleary-eyed writers who have written and rewritten countless times and make it shine. I have been fortunate to have Janis Whipple and Patti Smith to polish my work.

The cave dweller cannot thrive alone. For all who have rewarded my venturing forages with nourishment, I am thankful.

# INTRODUCTION

**D**id you know there is one habit you can develop that will make you happier? This same practice will make you healthier—and doesn't involve going to a gym. This simple routine strengthens your physical heart, improves your brain function, and elevates your mood. Your quality of life will flourish.

What is this secret to health and happiness? Giving thanks to God. The Bible reminds us often to thank God for our blessings, and with good reason. Researchers discovered that keeping a gratitude journal improves people's health and happiness. Once again, science proved that God's commands, including being thankful, are for our good (Deuteronomy 10:13).

Gratitude journaling transformed my life from a victim mentality to the victory of God's promises. Practicing intentional thankfulness obliterated my anxiety and bitterness and brought me peace and contentment.

I grew up in a strict religious home. My father used corporal punishment, as his father did with him. By age thirteen, I cried for days on end, blaming my parents for everything wrong. My tears dried with anger and bitterness as I rejected my parents' faith. I considered myself an atheist by age fifteen, and at sixteen became lost in drugs and continual fantasies of suicide. By age twenty, I hated my life and wanted to quit drugs, but didn't know how.

Philosophy intrigued me, so I read the New Testament to discover what Jesus, whom I esteemed as a philosopher, had to say about life. The claims Jesus made about Himself amazed me. "I am the bread of life." "I am the light of the world." "I am the way, the truth, and the life." *Either this guy was the most notorious con artist who ever lived,* I thought, *or he was telling the truth.* I decided to believe Him.

I carried my Bible everywhere and read it whenever I could—on the commute to and from work, while waiting at the bank, on breaks, and at home. I cried at Jesus' compassion when He healed people and forgave them. *Maybe he can forgive me too,* I thought.

I read, "Ask, and it will be given to you; seek, and you will find; knock, and it will be opened to you" (Luke 11:9). A "Dead End" sign appeared in my mind. I knew if I continued on my current path—high on marijuana from sunup to sundown—the only thing ahead for me was death. I said, "OK, God, please show me a group of people who can teach me how to live according to the Bible."

*Let's see if God can answer that one,* I thought. Within a couple of weeks, someone told me about a Bible study he attended. I asked him to take me there and had him draw me a map, in case he didn't show up.

I awoke the next day, filled with hope. For the first time in years, I didn't get high. Anticipation surged in my heart with the prospect of a new life. At the Bible study that evening, I devoured each word with ravenous hunger. The teacher said in passing, "If you confess with your mouth, 'Jesus is Lord,' and believe in your heart that God raised Him from the dead, you will be saved" (from Romans 10:9). I wanted to do that! When I returned home, I repeated those words and knew deep in my spirit that I believed. God saved me! I marveled at His mercy in rescuing a sinner like me.

Thankfulness filled my heart for God's goodness to me. I felt a "Holy Spirit high" far greater than that of marijuana, amphetamines, or LSD. I succumbed to the temptation of smoking marijuana one more time after attending the Bible studies, but that high was so depressing I determined never to do drugs again. Gratefulness to God bubbled in my heart with a joy no drug-induced euphoria could ever provide.

I told my friends about the Bible study group and what I was learning, but they called me a "Jesus freak." So I clung to people who loved God, didn't do drugs, and enjoyed praising the Lord with me.

I attended Bible classes, rejoicing with gratitude for God's goodness. One teacher talked about honoring our parents. He said, "If your parents were so bad, how did you turn out so good?" This question rocked my world. I forgave my parents and reconciled with them. I thanked God for the positives in my childhood, replacing hurtful experiences with pleasant memories.

I met a Christian man, Steve, and we married and started a family. I continued to thank God for my blessings, and we lived a wonderful life.

Over the years, however, my gratitude slipped into complacency as I forgot to be thankful. My former thought patterns—dwelling on negatives and complaining—resurfaced, sowing seeds of dissatisfaction and unhappiness. I shifted my blaming habit from my parents to my husband. Anger and bitterness took root in my heart, and I felt entitled to more in life—without him. After twenty-eight years of marriage, I left Steve and filed for divorce.

My failure to remain thankful for God's benefits led to the destruction of our family. My ingratitude snowballed into a downward spiral of despair and anxiety. Alone and anxious, I was unable to find peace. I sought prescription drugs to help me sleep.

I still read my Bible daily, crying out to God, "When will you heal my broken heart?" At a friend's suggestion, I listened to Bible teachings online. I devoured each word with ravenous hunger again.

In the middle of a teaching one day, the Lord burst into my thoughts with a revelation. He showed me how my divorce hurt me, my husband, our children, our church, and the community. I realized filing for divorce and tearing our family apart was far more egregious than my husband's mistakes and offenses. Horrified by my sin against so many people, I asked God to forgive me. In that revelatory moment, my anger toward Steve melted away, and I forgave him.

I felt an immense burden lift, and my broken heart healed. I called Steve and asked if we could meet and talk. At lunch the next day, I told him about my experience and how I repented for hurting him and others, and asked his forgiveness. He said, "Yes."

As we rose to leave, I blurted out something I didn't intend to say: "If you ever want to consider reconciliation, let me know." We both stood in silent shock at what I said. He replied, "I'll need to think about it."

In a couple of weeks, Steve called and said he'd be willing to start dating again. We sought out a Christian counselor who taught us communication skills.

Several months later, we remarried in the mountains of northeast Alabama, our first honeymoon site. Our three adult children were elated as we thanked God for bringing our family back together.

After we remarried, I discovered scientists were researching the benefits of gratitude journaling—improved health and happiness. I realized that ingratitude spiraled me into descending misery. Thankfulness, on the other hand, would be the garrison protecting my newfound happiness. I started keeping a gratitude journal, resolved to prevent my thoughts from eroding again into ingratitude, victimhood, entitlement, and bitterness.

I learned the hard way that ingratitude paves the road to destruction. God tells us about its grave consequences: "Because, although they knew God, they did not glorify Him as God nor were thankful, but became futile in their thoughts, and their foolish hearts were darkened" (Romans 1:21). "Unthankful" is one of the ungodly traits of people in the perilous last days (2 Timothy 3:1–5).

Writing what I'm thankful for is a powerful way to practice gratitude. The more I journal, the more I recognize the blessings that abound in my life.

As you write your blessings in this journal, you will discover the transforming power of giving thanks. I pray the scriptures, devotions, and quotes will inspire and motivate you to continue your gratitude journaling. May God bless your thanksgiving with abundant health and happiness.

# HOW TO USE YOUR GRATITUDE JOURNAL

Throughout these journal pages, you will find:

- Over a hundred scriptures about giving thanks, for inspiration.

- Lined spaces to list your thanks to God, with dates.

- Extra lined pages to write out additional prayers of thanksgiving and praise. It is helpful to date these entries for when you are reading back through your journal. When you need encouragement, this review will confirm how God has been good to you.

- Inspirational quotations on gratitude, especially from one of my favorite motivational speakers, Zig Ziglar.

- Biblical devotions for prayer and meditation in thankfulness, with space to write down personal reflections and prayers.

Upon waking, or thirty minutes before going to sleep at night, write down three to five things you are grateful for. If you miss a few days, don't get discouraged. Pick up your journal and resume writing. A new practice will take discipline until it becomes a habit. Anything worth having in life is worth the effort it takes to obtain it.

If you keep thanking God for the same things and need some inspiration and ideas, consult appendix A. This resource lists gratitude prompts in many categories of life.

To learn more about the scientific findings on gratitude journaling, consult appendix B, The Science of Gratitude. The research results will deepen your conviction that God cares for your welfare when He says to give thanks.

God bless you in your discovery of the transforming power of giving thanks.

## FREE GIFT!

Visit **judyransom.com** for a *free study guide* to *The Secret to Health and Happiness.* This guide will help you develop deeper gratitude, more forgiveness, and a closer relationship with God. Designed for individual study or a twelve-week small group Bible study.

*"Offer to God thanksgiving,*
*And pay your vows to the Most High.*
*Call upon Me in the day of trouble;*
*I will deliver you, and you shall glorify Me."*

**PSALM 50:14–15**

*Lord, today I am thankful for...*          DATE: ___/___/_____

_____
_____
_____
_____
_____
_____
_____
_____
_____
_____
_____
_____

*Lord, today I am thankful for...*          DATE: ___/___/_____

_____
_____
_____
_____
_____
_____
_____
_____
_____
_____
_____
_____

*Additional gratitude journaling and praise notes to God:*

*Enter into His gates with thanksgiving,*
*And into His courts with praise.*
*Be thankful to Him, and bless His name.*

**PSALM 100:4**

*Lord, today I am thankful for...*                    DATE: ___/___/_____

_____

_____

_____

_____

_____

_____

_____

_____

_____

_____

_____

*Lord, today I am thankful for...*                    DATE: ___/___/_____

_____

_____

_____

_____

_____

_____

_____

_____

_____

_____

_____

_____

*Additional gratitude journaling and praise notes to God:*

*Therefore by Him let us continually offer*
*the sacrifice of praise to God, that is, the fruit of our lips,*
*giving thanks to His name.*

**HEBREWS 13:15**

*Lord, today I am thankful for...*                    DATE: ___/___/_____

_____

_____

_____

_____

_____

_____

_____

_____

_____

_____

_____

*Lord, today I am thankful for...*                    DATE: ___/___/_____

_____

_____

_____

_____

_____

_____

_____

_____

_____

_____

_____

_____

*Additional gratitude journaling and praise notes to God:*

*Moreover David and the captains of the army separated for the service*
*some of the sons of Asaph, of Heman, and of Jeduthun, who should*
*prophesy with harps, stringed instruments, and cymbals… who*
*prophesied with a harp to give thanks and to praise the LORD.*

**1 CHRONICLES 25:1, 3**

*Lord, today I am thankful for…*                    DATE: ___/___/_____

_____

_____

_____

_____

_____

_____

_____

_____

_____

_____

_____

*Lord, today I am thankful for…*                    DATE: ___/___/_____

_____

_____

_____

_____

_____

_____

_____

_____

_____

_____

_____

*Additional gratitude journaling and praise notes to God:*

1

# TEN LEPERS HEALED

*One Made Whole*

D o you ever wonder why people don't say thank you anymore? When this topic comes up in conversation, my friends usually say it's because no one teaches manners anymore. However, I wonder if the problem is a lot older than that. Even Jesus was surprised by the ingratitude of a group of lepers He healed.

In the days before His passion and death, Jesus entered a village where ten lepers cried to Him, "Jesus, Master, have mercy on us!" (Luke 17:13). They were required by law to keep their distance from others due to their leprosy. If they ever did enter a public place, they had to call out, "Unclean! Unclean!" to warn people to stay away.

Imagine the plight of a leper in that culture. You're enjoying life with your family and community until the dreaded spots appear on your skin. The priest examines you, declares you unclean, and exiles you to live outside the village with other lepers. No more will you embrace your family or friends. You are a pariah, defiled, cut off from the life you once enjoyed.

Can you imagine the pleading and desperation in the voices of these ten lepers as they saw Jesus and called out to Him? Jesus exhibited no fear of their condition. He told them to go and show themselves to the priest. As they went, they were cleansed. The lepers continued on their way to the priest, who would declare them clean according to their law. They would now be free to go back to their families, to embrace and rejoin them. No more would people look at them in disgust and run from them to the cries of "Unclean! Unclean!" I can picture them breaking into a run at this point to find the priest.

Nine of them must have hurried on from the priest back to their homes. But to one of those healed, rejoining society wasn't his highest priority. He turned back to glorify God and thank Jesus. I can see him running in the opposite direction of the other nine, away from the priest, his family's embrace, and his community. He valued joining himself to the One who healed him much more highly than rejoining society. His priorities were correct, for he chose to commune in thanksgiving with the true High Priest.

Jesus was surprised that only one—a Samaritan despised by the Jews—returned to give thanks.

> So Jesus answered and said, "Were there not ten cleansed? But where are the nine? Were there not any found who returned to give glory to God except this foreigner?"
>
> **LUKE 17:17–18**

He said to this one healed man, "Arise, go thy way: thy faith hath made thee whole" (Luke 17:19, KJV). Nine lepers were healed of leprosy, but only one was made "whole," which means to be rescued, healed, and saved.

How often do we allow the things of this world to take priority over our communion with the Lord in offering Him praise and thanksgiving? How often do we settle for a few blessings when our heavenly Father wants to bless us more than we can ask or think? (Ephesians 3:20). He gave us the key to enjoy His fellowship and receive His goodness—to enter His presence with thanksgiving.

> Enter into His gates with thanksgiving, And into His courts with praise. Be thankful to Him, and bless His name.
>
> **PSALM 100:4**

*Reflections:*

*Giving thanks always for all things to God the Father*
*in the name of our Lord Jesus Christ.*

**EPHESIANS 5:20**

*Lord, today I am thankful for...*          DATE: ___/___/_____

_____

_____

_____

_____

_____

_____

_____

_____

_____

_____

_____

_____

*Lord, today I am thankful for...*          DATE: ___/___/_____

_____

_____

_____

_____

_____

_____

_____

_____

_____

_____

_____

_____

*Additional gratitude journaling and praise notes to God:*

*In everything give thanks; for this is the will of God
in Christ Jesus for you.*

**1 Thessalonians 5:18**

*Lord, today I am thankful for...*　　　　　　　　Date: ___/___/_____

_____

_____

_____

_____

_____

_____

_____

_____

_____

_____

_____

*Lord, today I am thankful for...*　　　　　　　　Date: ___/___/_____

_____

_____

_____

_____

_____

_____

_____

_____

_____

_____

_____

_____

*Additional gratitude journaling and praise notes to God:*

*Now when Daniel knew that the writing was signed, he went home.*
*And in his upper room, with his windows open toward Jerusalem,*
*he knelt down on his knees three times that day,*
*and prayed and gave thanks before his God,*
*as was his custom since early days.*

**DANIEL 6:10**

*Lord, today I am thankful for…*          DATE: ___/___/_____

_____

_____

_____

_____

_____

_____

_____

_____

_____

*Lord, today I am thankful for…*          DATE: ___/___/_____

_____

_____

_____

_____

_____

_____

_____

_____

_____

_____

*Additional gratitude journaling and praise notes to God:*

*Sing to the LORD with thanksgiving;*
*Sing praises on the harp to our God.*
**PSALM 147:7**

*Lord, today I am thankful for...*      DATE: ___/___/_____

_____

_____

_____

_____

_____

_____

_____

_____

_____

_____

*Lord, today I am thankful for...*      DATE: ___/___/_____

_____

_____

_____

_____

_____

_____

_____

_____

_____

_____

*Additional gratitude journaling and praise notes to God:*

*Gratitude is the healthiest of all human emotions. The more you express gratitude for what you have, the more likely you will have even more to express gratitude for.*

**ZIG ZIGLAR**

*Sing praise to the LORD, you saints of His,*
*And give thanks at the remembrance of His holy name.*

**PSALM 30:4**

*Lord, today I am thankful for...*          DATE: ___/___/_____

_____

_____

_____

_____

_____

_____

_____

_____

_____

_____

_____

*Lord, today I am thankful for...*          DATE: ___/___/_____

_____

_____

_____

_____

_____

_____

_____

_____

_____

_____

_____

*Additional gratitude journaling and praise notes to God:*

*I will give You thanks in the great assembly;*
*I will praise You among many people.*

**PSALM 35:18**

*Lord, today I am thankful for...*          DATE: ___/___/_____

_____

_____

_____

_____

_____

_____

_____

_____

_____

_____

_____

*Lord, today I am thankful for...*          DATE: ___/___/_____

_____

_____

_____

_____

_____

_____

_____

_____

_____

_____

_____

_____

*Additional gratitude journaling and praise notes to God:*

*So I brought the leaders of Judah up on the wall, and appointed*
*two large thanksgiving choirs.... The other thanksgiving choir*
*went the opposite way.... So the two thanksgiving choirs stood in*
*the house of God, likewise I and the half of the rulers with me.*

**NEHEMIAH 12:31, 38, 40**

*Lord, today I am thankful for...*                    DATE: ___/___/_____

_____

_____

_____

_____

_____

_____

_____

_____

_____

_____

_____

*Lord, today I am thankful for...*                    DATE: ___/___/_____

_____

_____

_____

_____

_____

_____

_____

_____

_____

_____

_____

*Additional gratitude journaling and praise notes to God:*

*Blessed be the Lord,*
*Who daily loads us with benefits,*
*The God of our salvation! Selah*

**PSALM 68:19**

*Lord, today I am thankful for...*                    DATE: ___/___/_____

_____

_____

_____

_____

_____

_____

_____

_____

_____

_____

_____

_____


*Lord, today I am thankful for...*                    DATE: ___/___/_____

_____

_____

_____

_____

_____

_____

_____

_____

_____

_____

_____

_____

_____

*Additional gratitude journaling and praise notes to God:*

# 2

# JOY IN HIS PRESENCE

## *Giving Thanks*

Our God is omnipresent, filling heaven and earth (Jeremiah 23:24). No matter where we go, He is present with us (Psalm 139:7–10; 46:1). Yet the scriptures speak of us entering into His presence.

> Serve the LORD with gladness;
> Come before His presence with singing....
> Enter into His gates with thanksgiving,
> And into His courts with praise.
> Be thankful to Him, and bless His name.
>
> **PSALM 100:2, 4**

God dwells in the spirit realm, which underlies and permeates everything we perceive with our senses in the physical domain (Acts 17:27–28; Colossians 1:17). While He is indeed everywhere present in the spirit, He calls us to draw near to Him, to be in His presence, where we can more easily hear His voice. The Lord's mouth is always by our ear, ready to speak His living Word of truth and wisdom into our heart and life (Matthew 4:4).

The distractions and cares of this world will keep us from God's presence—from hearing His voice of truth and love. Anxious worries, complaints, and fears fill our minds when we allow the things of this world to crowd out the spiritual realities and victories God has for us.

As we set aside some time from this world's busyness to commune with the Lord, who is always with us, He will gladly show us His solutions and fill us with His assurance and joy. A significant key to entering into the presence of God is thanksgiving. We can always find blessings to acknowledge and thank Him for in our lives.

> Let us come before His presence with thanksgiving;
> Let us shout joyfully to Him with psalms.
>
> PSALM 95:2

As we pause to give Him thanks, we can find rest in His presence, where the cares of this world will not shake us, and we can hear the Lord's guidance and have fullness of joy.

> I have set the LORD always before me;
> because he is at my right hand, I shall not be shaken.
> Therefore my heart is glad, and my whole being rejoices;
>
> …
>
> You make known to me the path of life;
> in your presence there is fullness of joy;
> at your right hand are pleasures forevermore.
>
> PSALM 16:8–9, 11 (ESV)

*Reflections:*

*Thanks be to God for His indescribable gift!*
**2 CORINTHIANS 9:15**

*Lord, today I am thankful for...*          DATE: ___/___/_____

_____
_____
_____
_____
_____
_____
_____
_____
_____
_____
_____
_____
_____
_____

*Lord, today I am thankful for...*          DATE: ___/___/_____

_____
_____
_____
_____
_____
_____
_____
_____
_____
_____
_____
_____
_____
_____

*Additional gratitude journaling and praise notes to God:*

*Therefore I also, after I heard of your faith in the Lord Jesus*
*and your love for all the saints, do not cease to give thanks*
*for you, making mention of you in my prayers.*

**EPHESIANS 1:15–16**

*Lord, today I am thankful for...*                    DATE: ___/___/_____

_____

_____

_____

_____

_____

_____

_____

_____

_____

_____

_____

*Lord, today I am thankful for...*                    DATE: ___/___/_____

_____

_____

_____

_____

_____

_____

_____

_____

_____

_____

_____

_____

*Additional gratitude journaling and praise notes to God:*

*Praise the LORD!*
*Oh, give thanks to the LORD, for He is good!*
*For His mercy endures forever.*

**PSALM 106:1**

*Lord, today I am thankful for...*                    DATE: ___/___/_____

_____

_____

_____

_____

_____

_____

_____

_____

_____

_____

*Lord, today I am thankful for...*                    DATE: ___/___/_____

_____

_____

_____

_____

_____

_____

_____

_____

_____

_____

*Additional gratitude journaling and praise notes to God:*

*We give thanks to God always for you all,*
*making mention of you in our prayers.*
### 1 Thessalonians 1:2

*Lord, today I am thankful for...*                    DATE: ___/___/_____

_____

_____

_____

_____

_____

_____

_____

_____

_____

_____

_____

*Lord, today I am thankful for...*                    DATE: ___/___/_____

_____

_____

_____

_____

_____

_____

_____

_____

_____

_____

_____

_____

_____

*Additional gratitude journaling and praise notes to God:*

*Gratitude is not only the greatest of virtues, but the parent of all the others.*

**MARCUS TULLIUS CICERO**

*But thanks be to God, who gives us the victory*
*through our Lord Jesus Christ.*
**1 Corinthians 15:57**

*Lord, today I am thankful for...*                DATE: ___/___/_____

_____
_____
_____
_____
_____
_____
_____
_____
_____
_____
_____
_____

*Lord, today I am thankful for...*                DATE: ___/___/_____

_____
_____
_____
_____
_____
_____
_____
_____
_____
_____
_____
_____

*Additional gratitude journaling and praise notes to God:*

*"We give You thanks, O Lord God Almighty,*
*The One who is and who was and who is to come,*
*Because You have taken Your great power and reigned."*
**REVELATION 11:17**

*Lord, today I am thankful for...*                    DATE: ___/___/_____

_____

_____

_____

_____

_____

_____

_____

_____

_____

_____

*Lord, today I am thankful for...*                    DATE: ___/___/_____

_____

_____

_____

_____

_____

_____

_____

_____

_____

_____

_____

*Additional gratitude journaling and praise notes to God:*

*For this reason we also thank God without ceasing, because*
*when you received the word of God which you heard from us,*
*you welcomed it not as the word of men, but as it is in truth,*
*the word of God, which also effectively works in you who believe.*

**1 THESSALONIANS 2:13**

*Lord, today I am thankful for...*          DATE: ___/___/_____

_____

_____

_____

_____

_____

_____

_____

_____

_____

_____

_____

*Lord, today I am thankful for...*          DATE: ___/___/_____

_____

_____

_____

_____

_____

_____

_____

_____

_____

_____

_____

*Additional gratitude journaling and praise notes to God:*

*And whatever you do in word or deed,*
*do all in the name of the Lord Jesus, giving thanks*
*to God the Father through Him.*

**COLOSSIANS 3:17**

*Lord, today I am thankful for...*          DATE: ___/___/_____

_____
_____
_____
_____
_____
_____
_____
_____
_____
_____
_____

*Lord, today I am thankful for...*          DATE: ___/___/_____

_____
_____
_____
_____
_____
_____
_____
_____
_____
_____
_____
_____

*Additional gratitude journaling and praise notes to God:*

# 3

# FORGET NOT ALL HIS BENEFITS

## *Or They'll Slip Away*

We may wonder at times if talking to ourselves is a sign we're crazy. However, we can find solace in knowing we're in good company, for King David did it often.

> Bless the LORD, O my soul,
> And forget not all His benefits.
>
> **PSALM 103:2**

David talked to himself, instructing his soul not to forget all of God's blessings. We too need to have a heart-to-heart with ourselves about not forgetting the Lord's countless benefits. The Hebrew word for *forget* in the above verse means "ignore, wither, to cease to care." The same word is used in Genesis.

> Yet the chief butler did not remember Joseph, but forgot him.
>
> **GENESIS 40:23**

The chief butler didn't care enough about Joseph, even after Joseph interpreted his dream and gave him the hope of deliverance. He didn't remember the promise he made to speak to Pharaoh on Joseph's behalf. He forgot how Joseph served him and showed concern for him while he was in prison (Genesis 40:4, 7). The butler must have been thrilled at his good fortune to remain alive and return to his trusted position with Pharaoh. Yet he forgot about Joseph for two long years, ceasing to care about what this young, godly man had done for him. As the butler ignored the kindness done to him, the memory of Joseph withered in his mind.

This word *forget* also occurs in Deuteronomy. When Moses gave final instructions before his death, he warned the children of Israel not to forget what God had done for them.

> Only be careful, and watch yourselves closely so that you do not forget the things your eyes have seen or let them fade from your heart as long as you live. Teach them to your children and to their children after them.
>
> DEUTERONOMY 4:9 (NIV)

God wants us to be on guard and keep watch over ourselves diligently, so we don't forget the things we've seen Him do for us. If we ignore God's benefits, they will wither in our minds till we no longer care about them for "as long as we live."

King David knew the antidote to forgetting the Lord's blessings and ceasing to care about them. He told himself to bless the Lord for all His benefits. Thankfulness will guard our hearts, so we do not let the Lord's blessings wither and fade in our memory, and consequently lose them.

Gratitude journaling will help us "be on guard" and "watch ourselves closely," so we don't forget what God has done for us. As we continue to write down the Lord's blessings, we will not forget His benefits and let them slip away. We will preserve them in our hearts for as long as we live.

*Reflections:*

*O wretched man that I am! Who will deliver*
*me from this body of death?*
*I thank God—through Jesus Christ our Lord!*
*So then, with the mind I myself serve the law of God,*
*but with the flesh the law of sin.*

**ROMANS 7:24–25**

*Lord, today I am thankful for...*                    DATE: ___/___/_____

_____

_____

_____

_____

_____

_____

_____

_____

_____

*Lord, today I am thankful for...*                    DATE: ___/___/_____

_____

_____

_____

_____

_____

_____

_____

_____

_____

_____

*Additional gratitude journaling and praise notes to God:*

*"I thank You and praise You,*
*O God of my fathers;*
*You have given me wisdom and might,*
*And have now made known to me what we asked of You,*
*For You have made known to us the king's demand."*

**DANIEL 2:23**

*Lord, today I am thankful for...*     DATE: ___/___/_____

_____
_____
_____
_____
_____
_____
_____
_____
_____
_____

*Lord, today I am thankful for...*     DATE: ___/___/_____

_____
_____
_____
_____
_____
_____
_____
_____
_____
_____
_____

*Additional gratitude journaling and praise notes to God:*

*"But I will sacrifice to You*
*With the voice of thanksgiving;*
*I will pay what I have vowed.*
*Salvation is of the Lord."*

**JONAH 2:9**

*Lord, today I am thankful for...*          DATE: ___/___/_____

_____
_____
_____
_____
_____
_____
_____
_____
_____
_____
_____
_____

*Lord, today I am thankful for...*          DATE: ___/___/_____

_____
_____
_____
_____
_____
_____
_____
_____
_____
_____
_____
_____

*Additional gratitude journaling and praise notes to God:*

*Greet Priscilla and Aquila, my fellow workers in Christ Jesus,*
*who risked their own necks for my life, to whom not only I*
*give thanks, but also all the churches of the Gentiles.*

**ROMANS 16:3–4**

*Lord, today I am thankful for...*                    DATE: ___/___/_____

_____

_____

_____

_____

_____

_____

_____

_____

_____

_____

_____

*Lord, today I am thankful for...*                    DATE: ___/___/_____

_____

_____

_____

_____

_____

_____

_____

_____

_____

_____

_____

_____

*Additional gratitude journaling and praise notes to God:*

*Among the things you can give and still keep are your word, a smile, and a grateful heart.*

**ZIG ZIGLAR**

*Now thanks be to God who always leads us in triumph*
*in Christ, and through us diffuses the fragrance*
*of His knowledge in every place.*

**2 CORINTHIANS 2:14**

*Lord, today I am thankful for...*                DATE: ___/___/_____

_____

_____

_____

_____

_____

_____

_____

_____

_____

_____

_____

*Lord, today I am thankful for...*                DATE: ___/___/_____

_____

_____

_____

_____

_____

_____

_____

_____

_____

_____

_____

*Additional gratitude journaling and praise notes to God:*

*But God be thanked that though you were slaves of sin,*
*yet you obeyed from the heart that form of doctrine*
*to which you were delivered.*

**ROMANS 6:17**

*Lord, today I am thankful for…*                    DATE: ___/___/_____

_____

_____

_____

_____

_____

_____

_____

_____

_____

_____

_____

_____

*Lord, today I am thankful for…*                    DATE: ___/___/_____

_____

_____

_____

_____

_____

_____

_____

_____

_____

_____

_____

_____

*Additional gratitude journaling and praise notes to God:*

*I thank my God upon every remembrance of you.*

**PHILIPPIANS 1:3**

*Lord, today I am thankful for...*          DATE: ___/___/_____

_____

_____

_____

_____

_____

_____

_____

_____

_____

_____

_____

*Lord, today I am thankful for...*          DATE: ___/___/_____

_____

_____

_____

_____

_____

_____

_____

_____

_____

_____

_____

_____

*Additional gratitude journaling and praise notes to God:*

*We are bound to thank God always for you, brethren,*
*as it is fitting, because your faith grows exceedingly,*
*and the love of every one of you all*
*abounds toward each other.*

**2 Thessalonians 1:3**

*Lord, today I am thankful for...*                    Date: ___/___/_____

_____

_____

_____

_____

_____

_____

_____

_____

_____

_____

_____

*Lord, today I am thankful for...*                    Date: ___/___/_____

_____

_____

_____

_____

_____

_____

_____

_____

_____

_____

_____

*Additional gratitude journaling and praise notes to God:*

4

# THE FRUIT OF THANKFULNESS

*Taste and See*

W hatever we give our attention to is what we become, whether good or bad. When we practice giving thanks, we focus on the good in our lives and become more thankful. The fruit of our lips becomes refreshing and life-giving, encouraging those around us.

The world bombards us with negativity. Without intentionally practicing gratitude, our attention and focus will effortlessly gravitate toward the evil around us. As we "go with the flow" of negativity, we turn negative. The fruit of our lips become words of darkness, and we drain and discourage those around us.

The scriptures reveal this principle of becoming what we focus on in our lives.

> But we all, with unveiled face, beholding as in a mirror the glory of the Lord, are being transformed into the same image from glory to glory, just as by the Spirit of the Lord.
>
> 2 Corinthians 3:18

As we read and meditate on the scriptures, we are transformed into the image of Christ. He is the living Word, and as we focus on Him, we become living epistles, known and read by all men (2 Corinthians 3:2).

David understood this principle and was intentional in what he would and would not allow himself to fix his attention on.

> I will not look with approval
> > on anything that is vile.
> I hate what faithless people do;
> > I will have no part in it.
>
> **PSALM 101:3 (NIV)**

Our adversary also understands this principle. As the prince of the power of the air (Ephesians 2:2), he seeks to lure our attention away from what the scriptures say we are in Christ. The Internet, television, and media become more vile in content every day, attempting to trap us in evil. Like David, we must be deliberate and committed to what we choose to give our attention. We can be aware of the evil surrounding us, but God's goodness must be our focus in overcoming evil.

Paul advised us in Philippians to meditate on the good.

> Finally, brethren, whatever things are true, whatever things are noble, whatever things are just, whatever things are pure, whatever things are lovely, whatever things are of good report, if there is any virtue and if there is anything praiseworthy—meditate on these things.
>
> **PHILIPPIANS 4:8**

When we develop the habit of giving thanks, we will be looking at what is virtuous and praiseworthy in our lives. Our thoughts and words will become filled with whatever is true, noble, just, pure, lovely, and of good report. We will become living epistles of God's goodness, giving those around us the option to partake in the delightful fruit we bear.

> Oh, taste and see that the LORD is good;
> Blessed is the man who trusts in Him!
>
> **PSALM 34:8**

*Reflections:*

*First, I thank my God through Jesus Christ for you all,*
*that your faith is spoken of throughout the whole world.*

**ROMANS 1:8**

*Lord, today I am thankful for...*                    DATE: ___/___/_____

_____

_____

_____

_____

_____

_____

_____

_____

_____

_____

_____

*Lord, today I am thankful for...*                    DATE: ___/___/_____

_____

_____

_____

_____

_____

_____

_____

_____

_____

_____

_____

*Additional gratitude journaling and praise notes to God:*

*I thank my God always concerning you for the grace of God
which was given to you by Christ Jesus.*

**1 Corinthians 1:4**

*Lord, today I am thankful for...*                    DATE: ___/___/_____

_____
_____
_____
_____
_____
_____
_____
_____
_____
_____
_____
_____

*Lord, today I am thankful for...*                    DATE: ___/___/_____

_____
_____
_____
_____
_____
_____
_____
_____
_____
_____
_____
_____
_____

*Additional gratitude journaling and praise notes to God:*

*But thanks be to God who puts the same earnest care*
*for you into the heart of Titus.*

**2 Corinthians 8:16**

*Lord, today I am thankful for...*        Date: ___/___/_____

_____

_____

_____

_____

_____

_____

_____

_____

_____

_____

*Lord, today I am thankful for...*        Date: ___/___/_____

_____

_____

_____

_____

_____

_____

_____

_____

_____

_____

*Additional gratitude journaling and praise notes to God:*

*We give thanks to the God and Father of our Lord Jesus Christ,*
*praying always for you.*
**COLOSSIANS 1:3**

*Lord, today I am thankful for...*                    DATE: ___/___/_____

_____
_____
_____
_____
_____
_____
_____
_____
_____
_____
_____

*Lord, today I am thankful for...*                    DATE: ___/___/_____

_____
_____
_____
_____
_____
_____
_____
_____
_____
_____
_____
_____

*Additional gratitude journaling and praise notes to God:*

*Feeling gratitude*

*and not expressing*

*it is like wrapping*

*a present and*

*not giving it.*

WILLIAM ARTHUR WARD

*We give thanks to You, O God, we give thanks!*
*For Your wondrous works declare that Your name is near.*

**PSALM 75:1**

*Lord, today I am thankful for...*                    DATE: ___/___/_____

_____

_____

_____

_____

_____

_____

_____

_____

_____

_____

_____

*Lord, today I am thankful for...*                    DATE: ___/___/_____

_____

_____

_____

_____

_____

_____

_____

_____

_____

_____

_____

*Additional gratitude journaling and praise notes to God:*

*And I thank Christ Jesus our Lord who has enabled me,*
*because He counted me faithful, putting me into the ministry.*
**1 TIMOTHY 1:12**

*Lord, today I am thankful for...*              DATE: ___/___/_____

_____
_____
_____
_____
_____
_____
_____
_____
_____
_____
_____

*Lord, today I am thankful for...*              DATE: ___/___/_____

_____
_____
_____
_____
_____
_____
_____
_____
_____
_____
_____
_____

*Additional gratitude journaling and praise notes to God:*

*"Now therefore, our God,*
*We thank You*
*And praise Your glorious name.*
*But who am I, and who are my people,*
*That we should be able to offer so willingly as this?*
*For all things come from You,*
*And of Your own we have given You."*

**1 Chronicles 29:13–14**

*Lord, today I am thankful for...*                    Date: ___/___/_____

_____

_____

_____

_____

_____

_____

_____

_____

_____

_____

*Lord, today I am thankful for...*                    Date: ___/___/_____

_____

_____

_____

_____

_____

_____

_____

_____

_____

_____

*Additional gratitude journaling and praise notes to God:*

*Let the redeemed of the LORD say so,*
*Whom He has redeemed from the hand of the enemy.*

**PSALM 107:2**

*Lord, today I am thankful for…*　　　　　　　　DATE: ___/___/_____

_____
_____
_____
_____
_____
_____
_____
_____
_____
_____
_____
_____

*Lord, today I am thankful for…*　　　　　　　　DATE: ___/___/_____

_____
_____
_____
_____
_____
_____
_____
_____
_____
_____
_____
_____

*Additional gratitude journaling and praise notes to God:*

# 5

# A VICTOR

## *Not a Victim*

It is impossible to have a victim mindset and be grateful at the same time. Merriam-Webster defines *victim mentality* as "the belief that one is always a victim: the idea that bad things will always happen to one." A victor, on the other hand, is a winner in any struggle.

Sadly, I wasted away my teenage years in anger and bitterness, blaming my parents for everything wrong. I considered myself a victim and was not thankful. One day I heard a Bible teacher say, "If your parents were so bad, how did you turn out so good?" This question shook me. I began thinking about the good things my parents instilled in me, becoming more thankful as a result.

If anyone ever had a right to think of himself as a victim, it was Joseph (Genesis 37, 39–50). His brothers threw him into a pit, plotted to kill him, and sold him as a slave. Carried away to Egypt, Joseph didn't whine or complain about what his brothers did. Instead, he excelled, becoming the head steward of Potiphar, captain of Pharaoh's guard.

I believe that Joseph had an attitude of gratitude, making the best of the most terrible circumstances. This mindset is what grateful people have. They don't meet adversity with complaints, blaming others, or thinking of themselves as victims. Their gratitude enables them to take stock of the good in their lives, to rise above adverse circumstances.

As an employer for over thirty-five years, I have watched thankful employees excel, while whining, victim-minded employees didn't. What a joy it is to work with grateful people. I believe this is why Potiphar promoted Joseph, entrusting him with his entire household.

Unfortunately, Joseph was betrayed by Potiphar's wife and thrown into prison. How many people would be filled with anger for such unjust imprisonment, especially after being betrayed by family and sold into slavery? How many of us would let bitterness grow in our hearts, thinking about those who wronged us, all while plotting revenge?

But not Joseph. He excelled in captivity, for the prison keeper set him in charge of the prison. What a relationship Joseph had with God! The Bible tells us that the Lord was with Joseph and caused him to prosper, even in prison (Genesis 39:23).

When you continue to count the Lord's blessings while enduring hardships, you draw closer to Him. Your trust in God grows as you "enter into His gates with thanksgiving, and into His courts with praise" (Psalm 100:4). Show me a thankful follower of the Lord Jesus, and I'll show you someone who is close to God.

Like Joseph, we can draw closer to God with thanksgiving. We will not be blaming others and plotting revenge when we consider our blessings.

> In everything give thanks; for this is the will of God in Christ Jesus for you.
>
> **1 Thessalonians 5:18**

We can nurture our relationship with God by giving Him thanks daily. This habit will help us seek the Lord's goodness in situations, rather than focus on evil. Through thanksgiving to God, we can be a victor in life, not a victim.

*Reflections:*

*First of all, then, I urge that supplications, prayers, intercessions,*
*and thanksgivings be made for all people,*
*for kings and all who are in high positions, that we may lead*
*a peaceful and quiet life, godly and dignified in every way.*
### 1 Timothy 2:1–2 (ESV)

*Lord, today I am thankful for...*                DATE: ___/___/_____

_____
_____
_____
_____
_____
_____
_____
_____
_____
_____
_____

*Lord, today I am thankful for...*                DATE: ___/___/_____

_____
_____
_____
_____
_____
_____
_____
_____
_____
_____
_____

*Additional gratitude journaling and praise notes to God:*

*Jerusalem—built as a city*
*that is bound firmly together,*
*to which the tribes go up,*
*the tribes of the* Lord,
*as was decreed for Israel,*
*to give thanks to the name of the* Lord.

**Psalm 122:3–4 (ESV)**

*Lord, today I am thankful for...*                    Date: ___/___/_____

_____

_____

_____

_____

_____

_____

_____

_____

_____

_____

*Lord, today I am thankful for...*                    Date: ___/___/_____

_____

_____

_____

_____

_____

_____

_____

_____

_____

_____

*Additional gratitude journaling and praise notes to God:*

*Giving thanks to the Father who has qualified us to be partakers*
*of the inheritance of the saints in the light.*

**Colossians 1:12**

*Lord, today I am thankful for...*  DATE: ___/___/_____

_____

_____

_____

_____

_____

_____

_____

_____

_____

_____

_____

*Lord, today I am thankful for...*  DATE: ___/___/_____

_____

_____

_____

_____

_____

_____

_____

_____

_____

_____

_____

_____

*Additional gratitude journaling and praise notes to God:*

*Surely the righteous shall give thanks to Your name;*
*The upright shall dwell in Your presence.*

**PSALM 140:13**

*Lord, today I am thankful for...*                    DATE: ___/___/_____

_____

_____

_____

_____

_____

_____

_____

_____

_____

_____

*Lord, today I am thankful for...*                    DATE: ___/___/_____

_____

_____

_____

_____

_____

_____

_____

_____

_____

_____

*Additional gratitude journaling and praise notes to God:*

*End the day*

*with gratitude.*

*There is someone,*

*somewhere that has*

*less than you.*

ZIG ZIGLAR

*I thank God, whom I serve with a pure conscience,*
*as my forefathers did, as without ceasing I remember you*
*in my prayers night and day.*

**2 Timothy 1:3**

*Lord, today I am thankful for...*                DATE: ___/___/_____

_____
_____
_____
_____
_____
_____
_____
_____
_____
_____

*Lord, today I am thankful for...*                DATE: ___/___/_____

_____
_____
_____
_____
_____
_____
_____
_____
_____
_____

*Additional gratitude journaling and praise notes to God:*

*I thank my God, making mention of you always in my prayers.*

**PHILEMON 1:4**

*Lord, today I am thankful for...*                    DATE: ___/___/_____

_____

_____

_____

_____

_____

_____

_____

_____

_____

_____

_____

*Lord, today I am thankful for...*                    DATE: ___/___/_____

_____

_____

_____

_____

_____

_____

_____

_____

_____

_____

_____

_____

*Additional gratitude journaling and praise notes to God:*

*Save us, L*ORD *our God,*
*and gather us from the nations,*
*that we may give thanks to your holy name*
*and glory in your praise.*
**P**SALM **106:47 (NIV)**

*Lord, today I am thankful for...*                    DATE: ___/___/_____

_____
_____
_____
_____
_____
_____
_____
_____
_____
_____
_____

*Lord, today I am thankful for...*                    DATE: ___/___/_____

_____
_____
_____
_____
_____
_____
_____
_____
_____
_____
_____

*Additional gratitude journaling and praise notes to God:*

*Oh, sing to the L*ORD *a new song!*
*For He has done marvelous things;*
*His right hand and His holy arm have gained Him the victory.*

**PSALM 98:1**

*Lord, today I am thankful for...*                    DATE: ___/___/_____

_____
_____
_____
_____
_____
_____
_____
_____
_____
_____
_____

*Lord, today I am thankful for...*                    DATE: ___/___/_____

_____
_____
_____
_____
_____
_____
_____
_____
_____
_____
_____
_____

*Additional gratitude journaling and praise notes to God:*

# 6

# GIVE THANKS

## *Not Complaints*

Have you ever noticed how delightful it is to work with someone who has an overall attitude of gratitude? Whatever they're working on, they give it their all. When problems arise, they take it in stride and focus on finding the solution. Being around them is energizing and encouraging because their positive words impart life.

Unfortunately, most of us also know what it's like to be around an unthankful person. Instead of support and encouragement, complaints and criticism pour from their lips. When problems arise, they place blame, rather than work on solutions. It is exhausting to be around ungrateful people because they drain the life out of us.

Imagine what it was like for Moses leading the children of Israel through the wilderness. God showed many signs in Egypt and delivered the Israelites from slavery by the hand of Moses. He brought them out of Egypt with great riches. Yet when they saw the Egyptian army pursuing them, they cried out to Moses, "Weren't there graves in Egypt? Why have you brought us out to die in the wilderness? It would have been better to remain slaves than to die out here!"

Instead of thanking God for all his miraculous signs and deliverance, they complained at the first sign of trouble. Throughout their wilderness journey, the Israelites daily witnessed God's miracles and provision—the cloud to lead them by day, the pillar by night, water in the desert, and manna every morning. Yet amid all this evidence of God's goodness, they still complained.

If God wants us to enter His gates with thanksgiving (Psalm 100:4), then complaining will keep us from enjoying His fellowship. The Israelites complained and separated themselves so far from God that they worshiped a golden calf, crediting it for bringing them out of Egypt. God told Moses, "Let Me alone, that My wrath may burn hot against them and I may consume them. And I will make of you a great nation" (Exodus 32:10). Moses pleaded with God and saved the rebellious Israelites. What a heart!

Moses was so close to God that the Lord spoke to him as a friend (Exodus 33:11). And of course, Moses was thankful. We can see this in Deuteronomy 6:10–12 when Moses warned the Israelites not to forget what God had done for them. We can learn much from Moses about not forgetting all the Lord has done for us.

> Therefore by Him let us continually offer the sacrifice
> of praise to God, that is, the fruit of our lips,
> giving thanks to His name.
> **HEBREWS 13:15**

*Reflections:*

*Be anxious for nothing, but in everything*
*by prayer and supplication, with thanksgiving,*
*let your requests be made known to God.*

**PHILIPPIANS 4:6**

*Lord, today I am thankful for...*                    DATE: ___/___/_____

_____

_____

_____

_____

_____

_____

_____

_____

_____

_____

_____

_____

*Lord, today I am thankful for...*                    DATE: ___/___/_____

_____

_____

_____

_____

_____

_____

_____

_____

_____

_____

_____

_____

*Additional gratitude journaling and praise notes to God:*

*Continue earnestly in prayer,*
*being vigilant in it with thanksgiving.*
**COLOSSIANS 4:2**

*Lord, today I am thankful for...*                    DATE: ___/___/_____

_____

_____

_____

_____

_____

_____

_____

_____

_____

_____

_____

_____

*Lord, today I am thankful for...*                    DATE: ___/___/_____

_____

_____

_____

_____

_____

_____

_____

_____

_____

_____

_____

_____

_____

*Additional gratitude journaling and praise notes to God:*

*And he appointed some of the Levites to minister*
*before the ark of the LORD, to commemorate, to thank,*
*and to praise the LORD God of Israel.*

**1 CHRONICLES 16:4**

*Lord, today I am thankful for...*        DATE: ___/___/_____

_____

_____

_____

_____

_____

_____

_____

_____

_____

_____

_____

*Lord, today I am thankful for...*        DATE: ___/___/_____

_____

_____

_____

_____

_____

_____

_____

_____

_____

_____

_____

_____

*Additional gratitude journaling and praise notes to God:*

*On that day David first delivered this psalm into the hand*
*of Asaph and his brethren, to thank the LORD:*
*Oh, give thanks to the LORD!*
*Call upon His name;*
*Make known His deeds among the peoples!*
**1 CHRONICLES 16:7–8**

*Lord, today I am thankful for...*          DATE: ___/___/_____

*Lord, today I am thankful for...*          DATE: ___/___/_____

*Additional gratitude journaling and praise notes to God:*

*Gratitude is*

*the fairest blossom*

*which springs*

*from the soul.*

**HENRY WARD BEECHER**

*I will sing of the mercies of the LORD forever;*
*With my mouth will I make known Your faithfulness*
*to all generations.*

**PSALM 89:1**

*Lord, today I am thankful for...*                    DATE: ___/___/_____

_____

_____

_____

_____

_____

_____

_____

_____

_____

_____

_____

*Lord, today I am thankful for...*                    DATE: ___/___/_____

_____

_____

_____

_____

_____

_____

_____

_____

_____

_____

_____

_____

_____

*Additional gratitude journaling and praise notes to God:*

*Oh, that men would give thanks to the* LORD *for His goodness,*
*And for His wonderful works to the children of men!*
*Let them sacrifice the sacrifices of thanksgiving,*
*And declare His works with rejoicing.*

**PSALM 107:21–22**

*Lord, today I am thankful for...*          DATE: ___/___/_____

_____

_____

_____

_____

_____

_____

_____

_____

_____

_____

_____

*Lord, today I am thankful for...*          DATE: ___/___/_____

_____

_____

_____

_____

_____

_____

_____

_____

_____

_____

_____

*Additional gratitude journaling and praise notes to God:*

*With praise and thanksgiving they sang to the LORD:*
*"He is good;*
*his love to Israel endures forever."*
*And all the people gave a great shout of praise to the LORD,*
*because the foundation of the house of the LORD was laid.*

**EZRA 3:11 (NIV)**

*Lord, today I am thankful for...*          DATE: ___/___/_____

_____

_____

_____

_____

_____

_____

_____

_____

_____

_____


*Lord, today I am thankful for...*          DATE: ___/___/_____

_____

_____

_____

_____

_____

_____

_____

_____

_____

_____

*Additional gratitude journaling and praise notes to God:*

*The Levites were Jeshua, Binnui, Kadmiel, Sherebiah, Judah,*
*and also Mattaniah, who, together with his associates,*
*was in charge of the songs of thanksgiving.*
**NEHEMIAH 12:8 (NIV)**

*Lord, today I am thankful for...*                    DATE: ___/___/_____

_____
_____
_____
_____
_____
_____
_____
_____
_____
_____
_____
_____

*Lord, today I am thankful for...*                    DATE: ___/___/_____

_____
_____
_____
_____
_____
_____
_____
_____
_____
_____
_____
_____
_____

*Additional gratitude journaling and praise notes to God:*

# 7

# IN EVERYTHING GIVE THANKS

## *Through Good and Bad*

*In everything give thanks; for this is the will
of God in Christ Jesus for you.*

**1 Thessalonians 5:18**

Think of all God's blessings—His salvation, hope, wisdom, guidance, direction, faithfulness, unconditional love, grace, provision, truth, protection, and deliverance. When we think of His abundant goodness, how can we not give Him thanks in everything?

A quote attributed to Epictetus, a Greek philosopher, says, "It's not what happens to you, but how you react to it that matters." How fitting, for he was born a slave. I like to practice this precept in simple daily events because it exercises and trains my mind for far weightier life crises.

If someone is driving slowly in front of me, I no longer grow impatient and angry, hurling cross words like I used to. This slow car could cause me to miss danger up ahead that I can't see. If I'm stuck in traffic and barely moving, I can use that time to get quiet and pray or sing praises to God. If an accident lies ahead of me on the road, I pray for those involved. I can use the time to have a positive spiritual impact wherever I am.

When I'm in a long checkout line at the store or waiting on a slow cashier, there's no point in getting angry or unkind. I can take the time to talk with people in line, make light of the situation, and share a little of God's love and goodness with those around me. Practicing positive reactions trains me to make the most of the present moment, with God at work within me. It's a lot less stressful to remain peaceful and content than to become impatient and angry.

God is holy, just, true, and faithful. He is not the author of confusion but of peace. Every good and perfect gift comes from Him. Christ became wisdom for us, and I seek that wisdom in life's matters, thanking God for showing me what's going on spiritually, what to do or not do, and what to say or not say.

I thank God for helping me to be patient and kind, make the best of any situation, and discern both good and evil. I can give Him thanks *in* everything, even when I am in the midst of spiritual darkness, for He is light, and He dwells within me.

> If I ascend into heaven, You are there;
> If I make my bed in hell, behold, You are there.
> If I take the wings of the morning,
> And dwell in the uttermost parts of the sea,
> Even there Your hand shall lead me,
> And Your right hand shall hold me.
>
> PSALM 139:8–10

Wherever we are, we are God's children and ambassadors for the Lord Jesus. We are salt and light in this world. No matter the circumstances, we can look to God, ask for His wisdom, and give Him thanks. A thankful heart keeps God in the picture with His encouragement and comfort. We can then share His encouragement and comfort with those around us. Praise the Lord! We can thank Him for calling us to represent Him on earth—in everything.

*Reflections:*

*And Hezekiah appointed the divisions of the priests and the Levites according to their divisions, each man according to his service, the priests and Levites for burnt offerings and peace offerings, to serve, to give thanks, and to praise in the gates of the camp of the LORD.*

**2 CHRONICLES 31:2**

*Lord, today I am thankful for...*                    DATE: ___/___/_____

_____

_____

_____

_____

_____

_____

_____

_____

_____

_____

_____

*Lord, today I am thankful for...*                    DATE: ___/___/_____

_____

_____

_____

_____

_____

_____

_____

_____

_____

_____

_____

*Additional gratitude journaling and praise notes to God:*

*Oh, give thanks to the LORD!*
*Call upon His name;*
*Make known His deeds among the peoples!*

**PSALM 105:1**

*Lord, today I am thankful for...*          DATE: ___/___/_____

_____

_____

_____

_____

_____

_____

_____

_____

_____

_____

_____

*Lord, today I am thankful for...*          DATE: ___/___/_____

_____

_____

_____

_____

_____

_____

_____

_____

_____

_____

_____

_____

_____

*Additional gratitude journaling and praise notes to God:*

*And let the peace of God rule in your hearts, to which also*
*you were called in one body; and be thankful.*

### COLOSSIANS 3:15

*Lord, today I am thankful for...*                     DATE: ___/___/_____

_____

_____

_____

_____

_____

_____

_____

_____

_____

_____

*Lord, today I am thankful for...*                     DATE: ___/___/_____

_____

_____

_____

_____

_____

_____

_____

_____

_____

_____

*Additional gratitude journaling and praise notes to God:*

*I will offer to You the sacrifice of thanksgiving,*
*And will call upon the name of the LORD.*

**PSALM 116:17**

*Lord, today I am thankful for...*          DATE: ___/___/_____

_____

_____

_____

_____

_____

_____

_____

_____

_____

_____

_____

*Lord, today I am thankful for...*          DATE: ___/___/_____

_____

_____

_____

_____

_____

_____

_____

_____

_____

_____

_____

*Additional gratitude journaling and praise notes to God:*

*Your gratitude attitude determines your life altitude.*

**ZIG ZIGLAR**

*Therefore I will give thanks to You, O L*ORD*, among the Gentiles,*
*And sing praises to Your name.*

**PSALM 18:49**

*Lord, today I am thankful for...*                    DATE: ___/___/_____

_____
_____
_____
_____
_____
_____
_____
_____
_____
_____
_____

*Lord, today I am thankful for...*                    DATE: ___/___/_____

_____
_____
_____
_____
_____
_____
_____
_____
_____
_____
_____

*Additional gratitude journaling and praise notes to God:*

*To the end that my glory may sing praise to You and not be silent.*
*O Lord my God, I will give thanks to You forever.*

**Psalm 30:12**

*Lord, today I am thankful for...*     Date: ___/___/_____

_____

_____

_____

_____

_____

_____

_____

_____

_____

_____

*Lord, today I am thankful for...*     Date: ___/___/_____

_____

_____

_____

_____

_____

_____

_____

_____

_____

_____

*Additional gratitude journaling and praise notes to God:*

*I will praise the name of God with a song,*
*And will magnify Him with thanksgiving.*
**PSALM 69:30**

*Lord, today I am thankful for...*  DATE: ___/___/_____

_____
_____
_____
_____
_____
_____
_____
_____
_____
_____
_____
_____

*Lord, today I am thankful for...*  DATE: ___/___/_____

_____
_____
_____
_____
_____
_____
_____
_____
_____
_____
_____
_____
_____

*Additional gratitude journaling and praise notes to God:*

*Rooted and built up in Him and established in the faith,*
*as you have been taught, abounding in it with thanksgiving.*
COLOSSIANS 2:7

*Lord, today I am thankful for...*                    DATE: ___/___/_____

*Lord, today I am thankful for...*                    DATE: ___/___/_____

*Additional gratitude journaling and praise notes to God:*

# 8

# THANKFUL FOR ONE ANOTHER

## *Even When It Isn't Easy*

I appreciate people who are thankful for me. They accept me and recognize my strengths while overlooking my shortcomings. They give praise and encouragement, and it's a joy to spend time with them. When they ask for help, I am eager to go above and beyond. I find their appreciation for me is energizing, infusing me with enthusiasm and creativity.

So it is with the gratitude we express toward others. When we focus on people's strengths and tell them why we're thankful for their positive qualities, they shine more brightly. People thrive in an atmosphere of acceptance and gratitude. Conversely, they wither in an atmosphere of criticism and disdain.

It can be challenging to consistently show gratitude for the people we live and work with—our spouse, children, relatives, roommates, and coworkers. We see their daily lives, warts and all, and they observe our faults as well. Will we focus on the positive qualities we're thankful for? Or will we slip into dwelling on the negatives? One attitude produces peace and joy, while the other breeds strife and discouragement.

When I am annoyed or angry with someone, I remind myself that Christ died for them. This perspective helps me see the love God has for them and why they are worthy of my love and acceptance. I can choose to focus on their faults and mistakes and drive myself crazy. Or I can dwell on their strengths and good qualities, making it easier to thank God for them. Then I can express why I'm grateful for them.

Magnifying people's positives isn't always easy, because we are at war in the spiritual realm. God is consistently for us. The god of this age—the accuser of the brethren—is always against us. We get to cast the deciding vote. We decide to love and be thankful or to criticize and judge. We choose who will rule us— the adversary or the Lord Jesus.

When we fall into the habit of focusing on someone's faults and shortcomings, it is difficult to see the good in them. God still loves them, yet we dole out judgment and criticism rather than love. We not only hurt them but ourselves more, for death and life are in the power of the tongue, and we will eat the fruit of our lips (Proverbs 18:21).

When faced with the temptation to criticize or complain about someone, I find it helpful to write down the person's strengths and qualities and focus on these instead of the bad. Every attribute has a positive and negative side. For example, messy people are usually easygoing and accepting of others. On the other hand, highly organized people may tend to be hard on themselves and others. It all depends on what we want to focus on—the good or the bad. When we dwell on the good, it is a lot easier to be thankful for those around us.

I thank my God upon every remembrance of you.

**PHILIPPIANS 1:3**

I thank my God always concerning you for the grace of God which was given to you by Christ Jesus.

**1 CORINTHIANS 1:4**

*Reflections:*

*Let us come before His presence with thanksgiving;*
*Let us shout joyfully to Him with psalms.*

**PSALM 95:2**

*Lord, today I am thankful for...*                    DATE: ___/___/_____

_____

_____

_____

_____

_____

_____

_____

_____

_____

_____

_____

_____

*Lord, today I am thankful for...*                    DATE: ___/___/_____

_____

_____

_____

_____

_____

_____

_____

_____

_____

_____

_____

_____

*Additional gratitude journaling and praise notes to God:*

*At midnight I will rise to give thanks to You,*
*Because of Your righteous judgments.*

**PSALM 119:62**

*Lord, today I am thankful for...*　　　　　　　DATE: ___/___/_____

_____
_____
_____
_____
_____
_____
_____
_____
_____
_____
_____

*Lord, today I am thankful for...*　　　　　　　DATE: ___/___/_____

_____
_____
_____
_____
_____
_____
_____
_____
_____
_____
_____

*Additional gratitude journaling and praise notes to God:*

*All the angels stood around the throne and the elders*
*and the four living creatures, and fell on their faces*
*before the throne and worshiped God, saying:*
*"Amen! Blessing and glory and wisdom,*
*Thanksgiving and honor and power and might,*
*Be to our God forever and ever. Amen."*

**REVELATION 7:11–12**

*Lord, today I am thankful for...*                    DATE: ___/___/_____

_____

_____

_____

_____

_____

_____

_____

_____

_____

_____

_____

_____

*Lord, today I am thankful for...*                    DATE: ___/___/_____

_____

_____

_____

_____

_____

_____

_____

_____

_____

_____

_____

_____

*Additional gratitude journaling and praise notes to God:*

*At that time Jesus answered and said, "I thank You, Father,*
*Lord of heaven and earth, that You have hidden these things*
*from the wise and prudent and have revealed them to babes."*

**MATTHEW 11:25**

*Lord, today I am thankful for...*          DATE: ___/___/_____

*Lord, today I am thankful for...*          DATE: ___/___/_____

*Additional gratitude journaling and praise notes to God:*

*Gratitude is an*
*offering precious in*
*the sight of God, and it*
*is one that the poorest*
*of us can make and be*
*not poorer but richer*
*for having made it.*

A. W. TOZER

*And the twenty-four elders who sat before God on their*
*thrones fell on their faces and worshiped God, saying:*
*"We give You thanks, O Lord God Almighty,*
*The One who is and who was and who is to come,*
*Because You have taken Your great power and reigned."*

**REVELATION 11:16–17**

*Lord, today I am thankful for...*                    DATE: ___/___/_____

_____

_____

_____

_____

_____

_____

_____

_____

_____

_____

*Lord, today I am thankful for...*                    DATE: ___/___/_____

_____

_____

_____

_____

_____

_____

_____

_____

_____

_____

*Additional gratitude journaling and praise notes to God:*

*You also must help us by prayer,*
*so that many will give thanks on our behalf*
*for the blessing granted us through the prayers of many.*
**2 CORINTHIANS 1:11 (ESV)**

*Lord, today I am thankful for...*          DATE: ___/___/_____

_____

_____

_____

_____

_____

_____

_____

_____

_____

_____

_____

*Lord, today I am thankful for...*          DATE: ___/___/_____

_____

_____

_____

_____

_____

_____

_____

_____

_____

_____

_____

*Additional gratitude journaling and praise notes to God:*

*And Jesus took the loaves, and when He had given thanks He distributed them to the disciples, and the disciples to those sitting down; and likewise of the fish, as much as they wanted.*

**JOHN 6:11**

*Lord, today I am thankful for...*　　　　　　　　DATE: ___/___/_____

_____

_____

_____

_____

_____

_____

_____

_____

_____

_____

*Lord, today I am thankful for...*　　　　　　　　DATE: ___/___/_____

_____

_____

_____

_____

_____

_____

_____

_____

_____

_____

_____

*Additional gratitude journaling and praise notes to God:*

*Then He took the cup, and gave thanks, and gave it*
*to them, saying, "Drink from it, all of you."*
**MATTHEW 26:27**

*Lord, today I am thankful for...*　　　　　　　　DATE: ___/___/_____

_____
_____
_____
_____
_____
_____
_____
_____
_____
_____
_____
_____

*Lord, today I am thankful for...*　　　　　　　　DATE: ___/___/_____

_____
_____
_____
_____
_____
_____
_____
_____
_____
_____
_____
_____
_____

*Additional gratitude journaling and praise notes to God:*

9

# THANKFUL OR ENTITLED?

*You Can't Be Both*

Have you ever given a gift to someone who acted like they were entitled to your offering? Did they thank you? Not a chance.

Thankfulness and entitlement stand at opposite poles of the response spectrum. Where there is gratitude, there is no sense of entitlement, and where there is an attitude of entitlement, there is no thankfulness.

When our children receive a gift, we usually prompt them with, "Now what do you say?" We want to teach them that the proper response to receiving a gift is to express gratitude.

Think about all the gifts our heavenly Father has bestowed upon us. How often do we remember to thank Him? He loads us daily with benefits (Psalm 68:19) and only tells us not to forget them all (Psalm 103:2).

Yet how many people give no thought to God's benefits? How many are living their lives as if the world owes them something? A sense of entitlement is rampant throughout our society and is growing. It must grieve God's heart to see so much ingratitude.

How can people learn to express gratitude? As the American poet Edgar A. Guest wrote, "I'd rather see a sermon than hear one any day." We must practice thanksgiving in our hearts and lives. Our attitude of gratitude will bring forth fruit that people will want to "taste and see that the Lord is good" (Psalm 34:8).

We need to take inventory of God's blessings and not forget to thank Him for all His benefits. Thankfulness will fill our hearts to overflowing to both God and man. We can teach our children to thank God and others and leave a legacy of gratitude.

> Blessed be the Lord,
> Who daily loads us with benefits,
> The God of our salvation! Selah

**PSALM 68:19**

*Reflections:*

*Then out of them shall proceed thanksgiving*
*And the voice of those who make merry;*
*I will multiply them, and they shall not diminish;*
*I will also glorify them, and they shall not be small.*

**JEREMIAH 30:19**

*Lord, today I am thankful for...*                    DATE: ___/___/_____

_____
_____
_____
_____
_____
_____
_____
_____
_____
_____

*Lord, today I am thankful for...*                    DATE: ___/___/_____

_____
_____
_____
_____
_____
_____
_____
_____
_____
_____

*Additional gratitude journaling and praise notes to God:*

*He who observes the day, observes it to the Lord;*
*and he who does not observe the day, to the Lord he does not observe*
*it. He who eats, eats to the Lord, for he gives God thanks; and he who*
*does not eat, to the Lord he does not eat, and gives God thanks.*

**ROMANS 14:6**

*Lord, today I am thankful for...*          DATE: ___/___/_____

_____
_____
_____
_____
_____
_____
_____
_____
_____
_____
_____

*Lord, today I am thankful for...*          DATE: ___/___/_____

_____
_____
_____
_____
_____
_____
_____
_____
_____
_____
_____

*Additional gratitude journaling and praise notes to God:*

*And when He had said these things, he took bread*
*and gave thanks to God in the presence of them all;*
*and when He had broken it He began to eat.*

**ACTS 27:35**

*Lord, today I am thankful for...*                    DATE: ___/___/_____

_____
_____
_____
_____
_____
_____
_____
_____
_____
_____
_____

*Lord, today I am thankful for...*                    DATE: ___/___/_____

_____
_____
_____
_____
_____
_____
_____
_____
_____
_____
_____
_____

*Additional gratitude journaling and praise notes to God:*

*And from there, when the brethren heard*
*about us, they came to meet us*
*as far as Appii Forum and Three Inns. When Paul saw them,*
*he thanked God and took courage.*

**ACTS 28:15**

*Lord, today I am thankful for...*                    DATE: ___/___/_____

_____

_____

_____

_____

_____

_____

_____

_____

_____

_____

_____

_____

*Lord, today I am thankful for...*                    DATE: ___/___/_____

_____

_____

_____

_____

_____

_____

_____

_____

_____

_____

_____

_____

*Additional gratitude journaling and praise notes to God:*

*Look back in*

*forgiveness,*

*forward in hope,*

down in compassion,

and up in gratitude.

**ZIG ZIGLAR**

*Both riches and honor come from You,*
*And You reign over all.*
*In Your hand is power and might;*
*In Your hand it is to make great*
*And to give strength to all.*
*Now therefore, our God,*
*We thank You*
*And praise Your glorious name.*

**1 CHRONICLES 29:12–13**

*Lord, today I am thankful for...*                    DATE: ___/___/_____

_____

_____

_____

_____

_____

_____

_____

_____

_____

*Lord, today I am thankful for...*                    DATE: ___/___/_____

_____

_____

_____

_____

_____

_____

_____

_____

_____

_____

*Additional gratitude journaling and praise notes to God:*

*And commanding to abstain from foods which God created*
*to be received with thanksgiving by those who believe and*
*know the truth. For every creature of God is good, and*
*nothing is to be refused if it is received with thanksgiving;*
*for it is sanctified by the word of God and prayer.*

**1 TIMOTHY 4:3–5**

*Lord, today I am thankful for...*          DATE: ___/___/_____

_____

_____

_____

_____

_____

_____

_____

_____

_____

_____

*Lord, today I am thankful for...*          DATE: ___/___/_____

_____

_____

_____

_____

_____

_____

_____

_____

_____

_____

_____

_____

*Additional gratitude journaling and praise notes to God:*

*Rejoice in the LORD, you righteous,*
*And give thanks at the remembrance of His holy name.*

**PSALM 97:12**

*Lord, today I am thankful for...*   DATE: ___/___/_____

_____
_____
_____
_____
_____
_____
_____
_____
_____
_____
_____
_____

*Lord, today I am thankful for...*   DATE: ___/___/_____

_____
_____
_____
_____
_____
_____
_____
_____
_____
_____
_____
_____

*Additional gratitude journaling and praise notes to God:*

*Oh, give thanks to the L*ORD*, for He is good!*
*For His mercy endures forever.*
*Oh, give thanks to the God of gods!*
*For His mercy endures forever.*
*Oh, give thanks to the Lord of lords!*
*For His mercy endures forever.*

**PSALM 136:1–3**

*Lord, today I am thankful for…*                    DATE: ___/___/_____

_____
_____
_____
_____
_____
_____
_____
_____
_____

*Lord, today I am thankful for…*                    DATE: ___/___/_____

_____
_____
_____
_____
_____
_____
_____
_____
_____
_____
_____

*Additional gratitude journaling and praise notes to God:*

# 10

# THE FORGIVING WAY TO GRATITUDE

*Not Easy, but Rewarding*

Every human relationship consists of imperfect people and requires forgiveness from time to time. Sometimes the offense is so hurtful that it is challenging to forgive. Yet we hurt ourselves the most when we fail to do so. Bitterness harbors a debt that no one can repay. The offender owes us, but cannot undo the wrong committed.

When we forgive, we release the offender from any debt toward us. Forgiveness is the only way to free ourselves from bitterness, which damages us spiritually, emotionally, and physically. Bitterness distances us from God, keeps us in the victim mindset of blaming others, and makes us physically ill. Unforgiveness is tantamount to taking poison and expecting the other person to die.

One of the biggest challenges in forgiveness is releasing our parents (or whoever raised us) from their debt toward us if we suffered abuse or neglect. We read God's command in Ephesians 6 and say, "That's not for me!"

> "Honor your father and mother," which is the first commandment with promise: "that it may be well with you and you may live long on the earth."
>
> **EPHESIANS 6:2–3**

I've lived on this earth for more than sixty years and have seen the same scenario play out in people's lives many times. Their parents wounded them as children, so they often speak badly of their parents, cursing them. Problems and ailments permeate their lives. Refusing to forgive our parents only brings trouble to ourselves, the opposite of Ephesians 6:3. It is not well with us, and we dig ourselves into an early grave.

I had a difficult childhood and suffered many things in life until I finally learned to forgive my parents from the heart. Remembering what God forgave me for was a big step toward forgiving them.

It helps to take inventory of the good in our lives. A lot of the positives we can identify in us are either because of or despite our parents. They either instilled virtues within us or gave us great resolve in what *not* to do or become. We can begin to make a list of the good in our lives, thanking God for those things.

In the process of forgiving our parents, we need to stop giving anger power over us. We are adults and can now take responsibility for our own lives. Being a victim or a victor is always a personal choice. We can choose to be free of the enslavement of deadly bitterness.

I was fortunate to reconcile with my parents and rebuild a relationship. But forgiveness does not always bring reconciliation. Sometimes we need to forgive people who would still do us harm in a relationship, therefore it is unwise to place our trust in them. However, we can release them of their debt toward us, and train ourselves to speak well of them—even if there's little we can say. We need to keep ourselves from speaking evil, for curses pouring from our lips only bring us death (Proverbs 18:21).

When Jesus told the disciples to keep forgiving someone (Luke 17:3–6), they responded, "Lord, increase our faith!" We can ask God to help us forgive. When we put away prideful bitterness and are humble before Him, He will give us the grace we need to forgive from our hearts. We can thank God for the blessings in our lives and be free from the victim mindset trap.

> Therefore, as God's chosen people, holy and dearly loved, clothe yourselves with compassion, kindness, humility, gentleness and patience. Bear with each other and forgive one another if any of you has a grievance against someone. Forgive as the Lord forgave you.
>
> COLOSSIANS 3:12–13 (NIV)

*Reflections:*

*You will be enriched in every way so that you can be generous*
*on every occasion, and through us your generosity will result*
*in thanksgiving to God. This service that you perform is*
*not only supplying the needs of the Lord's people but is also*
*overflowing in many expressions of thanks to God.*

**2 CORINTHIANS 9:11–12 (NIV)**

*Lord, today I am thankful for...*                    DATE: ___/___/_____

_____

_____

_____

_____

_____

_____

_____

_____

_____

*Lord, today I am thankful for...*                    DATE: ___/___/_____

_____

_____

_____

_____

_____

_____

_____

_____

_____

_____

*Additional gratitude journaling and praise notes to God:*

*For by the last words of David the Levites were numbered from twenty years old and above; because their duty was to help the sons of Aaron in the service of the house of the LORD, in the courts and in the chambers… to stand every morning to thank and praise the LORD, and likewise at evening.*

**1 CHRONICLES 23:27–28, 30**

*Lord, today I am thankful for…*                    DATE: ___/___/_____

_____

_____

_____

_____

_____

_____

_____

_____

_____

_____

*Lord, today I am thankful for…*                    DATE: ___/___/_____

_____

_____

_____

_____

_____

_____

_____

_____

_____

_____

_____

_____

*Additional gratitude journaling and praise notes to God:*

*Bless the LORD, O my soul;*
*And all that is within me, bless His holy name!*
*Bless the LORD, O my soul,*
*And forget not all His benefits:*
*Who forgives all your iniquities,*
*Who heals all your diseases,*
*Who redeems your life from destruction,*
*Who crowns you with lovingkindness and tender mercies.*

### PSALM 103:1–4

*Lord, today I am thankful for...*        DATE: ___/___/_____

_____

_____

_____

_____

_____

_____

_____

_____

*Lord, today I am thankful for...*        DATE: ___/___/_____

_____

_____

_____

_____

_____

_____

_____

_____

_____

_____

*Additional gratitude journaling and praise notes to God:*

*Indeed it came to pass, when the trumpeters and singers were as one,*
*to make one sound to be heard in praising and thanking the* LORD,
*and when they lifted up their voice with the trumpets and cymbals*
*and instruments of music, and praised the* LORD, *saying:*
*"For He is good, for His mercy endures forever,"*
*that the house, the house of the* LORD, *was filled with a cloud.*

## 2 CHRONICLES 5:13

*Lord, today I am thankful for…*                     DATE: ___/___/_____

_____

_____

_____

_____

_____

_____

_____

_____

_____

_____

*Lord, today I am thankful for…*                     DATE: ___/___/_____

_____

_____

_____

_____

_____

_____

_____

_____

_____

_____

*Additional gratitude journaling and praise notes to God:*

*Gratitude changes*

*the pangs*

*of memory into*

*a tranquil joy.*

**DIETRICH BONHOEFFER**

*"And you shall remember the L*ORD *your God, for it is He*
*who gives you power to get wealth, that He may establish*
*His covenant which He swore to your fathers, as it is this day."*

**DEUTERONOMY 8:18**

*Lord, today I am thankful for...*          DATE: ___/___/_____

_____
_____
_____
_____
_____
_____
_____
_____
_____
_____
_____

*Lord, today I am thankful for...*          DATE: ___/___/_____

_____
_____
_____
_____
_____
_____
_____
_____
_____
_____
_____
_____

*Additional gratitude journaling and praise notes to God:*

*And one of them, when he saw that he was healed, returned,*
*and with a loud voice glorified God, and fell down on his face*
*at His feet, giving Him thanks. And he was a Samaritan.*

**LUKE 17:15–16**

*Lord, today I am thankful for...*                    DATE: ___/___/_____

_____

_____

_____

_____

_____

_____

_____

_____

_____

_____

_____

_____

*Lord, today I am thankful for...*                    DATE: ___/___/_____

_____

_____

_____

_____

_____

_____

_____

_____

_____

_____

_____

_____

*Additional gratitude journaling and praise notes to God:*

*My mouth shall tell of Your righteousness*
*And Your salvation all the day,*
*For I do not know their limits.*

**Psalm 71:15**

*Lord, today I am thankful for...*　　　　　　Date: ___/___/_____

_____

_____

_____

_____

_____

_____

_____

_____

_____

_____

_____

*Lord, today I am thankful for...*　　　　　　Date: ___/___/_____

_____

_____

_____

_____

_____

_____

_____

_____

_____

_____

_____

_____

*Additional gratitude journaling and praise notes to God:*

*My lips shall greatly rejoice when I sing to You,*
*And my soul, which You have redeemed.*
*My tongue also shall talk of Your righteousness all the day long.*

**PSALM 71:23–24**

*Lord, today I am thankful for...*       DATE: ___/___/_____

*Lord, today I am thankful for...*       DATE: ___/___/_____

*Additional gratitude journaling and praise notes to God:*

# 11

# GRATITUDE POSITIONING SYSTEM

## *The GPS That Always Works!*

When we give thanks to the Lord, we position ourselves in a blossoming relationship with Him that grows sweeter every day. Thanking God for His blessings is our acknowledgment of His faithful love, grace, mercy, provision, and protection. Gratitude demonstrates that we don't take the Lord for granted and keeps our relationship with Him healthy and alive with growth.

When we express thanks to God, we recognize that all our blessings are from Him. We don't walk around with a chip on our shoulder, thinking God or the world owes us anything. Nor do we proclaim we are self-made men and women, for we recognize God provided everything we have. In this position of humility before the Father, He responds with grace—His unmerited favor. He blesses us not because we deserve it but because it is His good pleasure to bless those who submit to His loving care and provision.

With an attitude of gratitude, life's challenges won't blindside us. Instead, our thankful mindset conditions us to fix our minds upon God's blessings and solutions.

We bring glory to God when we give Him thanks. Every time you share what God has done for you, thanksgiving in your heart gives glory to God.

The apostle Paul suffered many afflictions for Christ. However, his Gratitude Positioning System kept him praising God despite being hard-pressed on every side, perplexed, persecuted, and struck down. He praised God's excellent power that he was not crushed, in despair, forsaken, or destroyed.

> But we have this treasure in earthen vessels, that the excellence of the power may be of God and not of us. We are hard-pressed on every side, yet not crushed; we are perplexed, but not in despair; persecuted, but not forsaken; struck down, but not destroyed.
>
> 2 CORINTHIANS 4:7–9

How would you like to have a GPS like that? We flip the switch "on" when we humbly position ourselves in gratitude to God. Even in hard times, we can look at what didn't happen and praise Him. The good Lord then pours out His grace to us. I believe that grace is the spiritual enablement to do what we absolutely cannot do in our flesh alone. By God's grace, we can come through the valleys in life and praise Him. Who *doesn't* need this kind of GPS in life?

Paul beautifully summed up his ministry with grace, thanksgiving, and glory to God.

> For all things are for your sakes, that grace, having spread through the many, may cause thanksgiving to abound to the glory of God.
>
> 2 CORINTHIANS 4:15

Thanksgiving positions us to receive God's provision, protection, and resilience through difficult times. This GPS will always work, directing us closer and closer to God.

*Reflections:*

*So we, Your people and sheep of Your pasture,*
*Will give You thanks forever;*
*We will show forth Your praise to all generations.*

**PSALM 79:13**

*Lord, today I am thankful for...*　　　　　　　DATE: ___/___/_____

_____
_____
_____
_____
_____
_____
_____
_____
_____
_____
_____

*Lord, today I am thankful for...*　　　　　　　DATE: ___/___/_____

_____
_____
_____
_____
_____
_____
_____
_____
_____
_____
_____
_____

*Additional gratitude journaling and praise notes to God:*

*This will be written for the generation to come,*
*That a people yet to be created may praise the Lord.*

**PSALM 102:18**

*Lord, today I am thankful for...*　　　　　　　　Date: ___/___/_____

_____

_____

_____

_____

_____

_____

_____

_____

_____

_____

_____

_____

*Lord, today I am thankful for...*　　　　　　　　Date: ___/___/_____

_____

_____

_____

_____

_____

_____

_____

_____

_____

_____

_____

_____

*Additional gratitude journaling and praise notes to God:*

*It is good to give thanks to the* LORD,
*And to sing praises to Your name, O Most High;*
*To declare Your lovingkindness in the morning,*
*And Your faithfulness every night,*
*On an instrument of ten strings,*
*On the lute,*
*And on the harp,*
*With harmonious sound.*

### PSALM 92:1–3

*Lord, today I am thankful for...*          DATE: ___/___/_____

_____
_____
_____
_____
_____
_____
_____
_____
_____
_____

*Lord, today I am thankful for...*          DATE: ___/___/_____

_____
_____
_____
_____
_____
_____
_____
_____
_____
_____
_____

*Additional gratitude journaling and praise notes to God:*

*For You, LORD, have made me glad through Your work;*
*I will triumph in the works of Your hands.*
*O LORD, how great are Your works!*
**PSALM 92:4–5**

*Lord, today I am thankful for...*          DATE: ___/___/_____

_____
_____
_____
_____
_____
_____
_____
_____
_____
_____
_____

*Lord, today I am thankful for...*          DATE: ___/___/_____

_____
_____
_____
_____
_____
_____
_____
_____
_____
_____
_____

*Additional gratitude journaling and praise notes to God:*

*You'll never meet a happy ungrateful person, or an unhappy grateful person because gratitude and happiness go together.*

**ZIG ZIGLAR**

*You have dealt well with Your servant,*
*O LORD, according to Your word.*
*Accept, I pray, the freewill offerings of my mouth, O LORD,*
*And teach me Your judgments.*

**PSALM 119:65, 108**

*Lord, today I am thankful for...*          DATE: ___/___/_____

_____

_____

_____

_____

_____

_____

_____

_____

_____

_____

_____

*Lord, today I am thankful for...*          DATE: ___/___/_____

_____

_____

_____

_____

_____

_____

_____

_____

_____

_____

*Additional gratitude journaling and praise notes to God:*

*Oh, give thanks to the God of heaven!*
*For His mercy endures forever.*
**PSALM 136:26**

*Lord, today I am thankful for...*            DATE: ___/___/_____

_____
_____
_____
_____
_____
_____
_____
_____
_____
_____
_____

*Lord, today I am thankful for...*            DATE: ___/___/_____

_____
_____
_____
_____
_____
_____
_____
_____
_____
_____
_____

*Additional gratitude journaling and praise notes to God:*

*For what thanks can we render to God for you, for all the joy*
*with which we rejoice for your sake before our God.*
**1 Thessalonians 3:9**

*Lord, today I am thankful for...*          DATE: ___/___/_____

_____
_____
_____
_____
_____
_____
_____
_____
_____
_____
_____

*Lord, today I am thankful for...*          DATE: ___/___/_____

_____
_____
_____
_____
_____
_____
_____
_____
_____
_____
_____

*Additional gratitude journaling and praise notes to God:*

*That I may proclaim with the voice of thanksgiving,*
*And tell of all Your wondrous works.*
**PSALM 26:7**

*Lord, today I am thankful for...*                    DATE: ___/___/_____

_____
_____
_____
_____
_____
_____
_____
_____
_____
_____
_____

*Lord, today I am thankful for...*                    DATE: ___/___/_____

_____
_____
_____
_____
_____
_____
_____
_____
_____
_____
_____
_____

*Additional gratitude journaling and praise notes to God:*

# 12

# I DIDN'T KNOW WHAT I HAD

## *Till It Was Gone*

I'm not proud to write this, but I was unthankful for my husband for many years, not knowing what I had till it was gone. During the four years of our separation and divorce, I began to realize how much we complemented one another—our interests, likes, dislikes, and personalities.

I thank God for His mercy in bringing us back together. Since then, we've been closer than ever. God helped us hit the "reset" button, with all things new in Christ.

> Therefore, if anyone is in Christ, he is a new creation; old things have passed away; behold, all things have become new.
>
> 2 CORINTHIANS 5:17

When we remarried, it was challenging at first to believe this promise—that we were a new creation in Christ, with old things passed away. If one of us complained, "You always do that," the other would need to respond, "That's in the past." Our fleshly weaknesses may still be with us, but the complaining and criticism are in the past.

We have learned to thank God for what we love about each other. Our shortcomings are why we need the fruit of the Spirit—especially patience, kindness, and goodness.

> But the fruit of the Spirit is love, joy, peace, patience, kindness, goodness,
> faithfulness, gentleness, self-control; against such things there is no law.
> **GALATIANS 5:22–23 (ESV)**

The fruit of the Spirit is not something we can create in ourselves. The spiritual fruit we bear in our Christian walk is a work of the Holy Spirit within us. Only God can produce a fruitful increase in our lives as we obey His Word and yield to the Spirit.

For example, if my husband says something hurtful to me, I have a choice. I can succumb to my carnal desire and become angry. Or I can look at the situation spiritually, with the love of God. Maybe he's tired or had a bad day. I can pray for him and ask if something is bothering him. This caring response is the Holy Spirit bearing fruit in my life—love, patience, kindness, and goodness.

Our labor of love is to speak and act according to God's Word, even when it isn't easy. As we obey God, the Holy Spirit works within us to bear fruit.

> "If you abide in Me, and My words abide in you, you will ask what
> you desire, and it shall be done for you. By this My Father is glorified,
> that you bear much fruit; so you will be My disciples."
> **JOHN 15:7–8**

As Steve and I endeavor to walk by the Spirit and not by the flesh, we enjoy more harmony with each other. We now realize we are best friends and soul mates, thanks to God's gracious work within us.

Focusing on the flesh and not being thankful for what I had—a husband who loved God—led to the destruction of our marriage and family. When I dwelled on fleshly weaknesses, they became magnified in my heart. It's easy to focus on sin. The real work lies in looking at God's spiritual reasons for loving the other person in a relationship.

Gratitude journaling keeps what I have—God's blessings—at the forefront of my mind. Thanksgiving guards my heart against carnal complaints and criticism. I pray that you learn from my mistakes and acknowledge God's benefits in your life with thanksgiving.

> Bless the LORD, O my soul, And forget not all His benefits.
> **PSALM 103:2**

*Reflections:*

*Therefore I will give thanks to You, O LORD, among the Gentiles,*
*And sing praises to Your name.*
**2 SAMUEL 22:50**

*Lord, today I am thankful for...*                    DATE: ___/___/_____

_____
_____
_____
_____
_____
_____
_____
_____
_____
_____
_____
_____

*Lord, today I am thankful for...*                    DATE: ___/___/_____

_____
_____
_____
_____
_____
_____
_____
_____
_____
_____
_____
_____
_____

*Additional gratitude journaling and praise notes to God:*

*Oh, give thanks to the LORD, for He is good!*
*For His mercy endures forever.*

**1 CHRONICLES 16:34**

*Lord, today I am thankful for...*                    DATE: ___/___/_____

_____

_____

_____

_____

_____

_____

_____

_____

_____

_____

_____

*Lord, today I am thankful for...*                    DATE: ___/___/_____

_____

_____

_____

_____

_____

_____

_____

_____

_____

_____

_____

*Additional gratitude journaling and praise notes to God:*

*Say also:*
*"Save us, O God of our salvation,*
*and gather and deliver us from among the nations,*
*that we may give thanks to your holy name*
*and glory in your praise."*

**1 CHRONICLES 16:35 (ESV)**

*Lord, today I am thankful for...*                    DATE: ___/___/_____

_____

_____

_____

_____

_____

_____

_____

_____

_____

*Lord, today I am thankful for...*                    DATE: ___/___/_____

_____

_____

_____

_____

_____

_____

_____

_____

_____

_____

*Additional gratitude journaling and praise notes to God:*

*With them were Heman and Jeduthun and the rest of those chosen*
*and expressly named to give thanks to the LORD,*
*for his steadfast love endures forever.*

**1 CHRONICLES 16:41 (ESV)**

*Lord, today I am thankful for...*                    DATE: ___/___/_____

*Lord, today I am thankful for...*                    DATE: ___/___/_____

*Additional gratitude journaling and praise notes to God:*

*The discipline of gratitude is the explicit effort to acknowledge that all I am and have is given to me as a gift of love, a gift to be celebrated with joy.*

**HENRI NOUWEN**

*Then Hezekiah said, "You have now dedicated yourselves
to the LORD. Come and bring sacrifices and thank offerings
to the temple of the LORD."
So the assembly brought sacrifices and thank offerings.*
2 CHRONICLES 29:31 (NIV)

*Lord, today I am thankful for...*  DATE: ___/___/_____

_____
_____
_____
_____
_____
_____
_____
_____
_____

*Lord, today I am thankful for...*  DATE: ___/___/_____

_____
_____
_____
_____
_____
_____
_____
_____
_____
_____
_____

*Additional gratitude journaling and praise notes to God:*

*Whenever the living creatures give glory and honor and thanks*
*to Him who sits on the throne, who lives forever and ever, the*
*twenty-four elders fall down before Him who sits on the throne*
*and worship Him… and cast their crowns before the throne.*

**REVELATION 4:9–10**

*Lord, today I am thankful for…*                    DATE: ___/___/_____

_____

_____

_____

_____

_____

_____

_____

_____

_____

_____

_____

*Lord, today I am thankful for…*                    DATE: ___/___/_____

_____

_____

_____

_____

_____

_____

_____

_____

_____

_____

*Additional gratitude journaling and praise notes to God:*

*And the leaders of the Levites… and their associates,*
*who stood opposite them to give praise and thanksgiving,*
*one section responding to the other, as prescribed*
*by David the man of God.*
**NEHEMIAH 12:24 (NIV)**

*Lord, today I am thankful for…*                    DATE: ___/___/_____

_____
_____
_____
_____
_____
_____
_____
_____
_____
_____

*Lord, today I am thankful for…*                    DATE: ___/___/_____

_____
_____
_____
_____
_____
_____
_____
_____
_____
_____
_____

*Additional gratitude journaling and praise notes to God:*

*But we are bound to give thanks to God always for you,*
*brethren beloved by the Lord, because God from the beginning*
*chose you for salvation through sanctification*
*by the Spirit and belief in the truth.*

**2 THESSALONIANS 2:13**

*Lord, today I am thankful for...*                    DATE: ___/___/_____

_____

_____

_____

_____

_____

_____

_____

_____

_____

_____

*Lord, today I am thankful for...*                    DATE: ___/___/_____

_____

_____

_____

_____

_____

_____

_____

_____

_____

_____

*Additional gratitude journaling and praise notes to God:*

# GRATITUDE PROMPTS

L isted here are some gratitude prompts to help you remember blessings, people, and events in your life for which you can give thanks to God. They are grouped into various categories. As you think of more prompts, add them to this list. Gratitude prompts will help you on those days when you need a gentle reminder of all you have to be thankful for in your life.

## 1. Spiritual

- People in my life who sowed seeds that brought me into relationship with God, and what those precious seeds were (words, acts of kindness)

- People who taught me the scriptures (memorable teachings and lessons learned)

- Ways in which God undeniably showed His love for me and blessed me

- Ways in which God has spoken to me personally (through His Word, through people, through other sources and experiences)

- Times when God saved my life

- How God healed me (physically, emotionally, mentally)

- Times of God's deliverance in my life (from spiritual oppression or affliction)

- Times God inspired me to help others

- Times God worked within me to speak His Word of life to someone in need

- Times God worked within me to bring healing to others

- Gifts and abilities the Lord has given me that help and bless others

- Desires God placed in my heart to do His will

- My church, pastors, spiritual teachers, and mentors

- Times the Lord corrected me because of His great love for me

- Times God made things work together for good, turning my lemons into lemonade

## 2. Physical

- The health I enjoy

- Physical strength enabling me to do various tasks

- Physical abilities I have to accomplish personal goals

- Physical and mental aspects of my life that help me excel

- Physical mobility, whether on my own or mechanical

- Ways in which doctors and other health professionals helped me

- Foods I enjoy that help me be stronger and healthier

- People who taught me how to be stronger and healthier

- Coaches who taught and encouraged me

- Organizations and publications that helped me become stronger and healthier

- Times of sweet sleep, and people or aids that helped me sleep better

## 3. Emotional

- Times and ways in which God healed my broken heart

- Relationships that were reconciled or greatly improved

- People who showed me support and encouragement

- Comments from people that lifted me

- Compliments I received from others

- People, organizations, and books that were instrumental in bringing me emotional healing

- People in my support circle now, and throughout various times in my life

- People who forgave me

- Times I forgave others

- Pets I loved and enjoyed caring for

- Positive things about people in my neighborhood

- Fun times I had with others

- Times I laughed real hard with friends

- Times I could offer comfort and encouragement to others

## 4. Intellectual

- Wonderful teachers throughout my life

- Things I learned from others

- Schools, organizations, and various media that helped me learn

- Strengths and abilities God gave me in different areas of knowledge

- People who encouraged me in my studies when I lacked confidence or was discouraged

- Subjects that thrill me to learn more about

- Ways in which I've taught others what I've learned

- Ways in which I've improved people's lives by sharing what I've learned

## 5. Psychological

- People who helped me overcome psychological difficulties and/or disorders

- People who helped me with learning disabilities

- Ways in which people helped me learn social skills

- Activities that help me relieve stress

- People and various media that helped me better deal with stress

- Music, composers, and songwriters who helped me relax and be peaceful

- Favorite places that helped me find calm and peace

- Things I learned and applied in overcoming anxiety

## 6. Material

- Clothing that is comfortable or makes me feel great

- Modern conveniences that provide warmth and cooling

- Basic needs of life I take for granted that not everyone is fortunate enough to have

- A roof over my head

- Favorite rooms, such as my bedroom, study, kitchen, living room

- My car, bike, and/or other means of transportation

- Appliances that save time and help me accomplish more

- Electronics that help me accomplish what I need to do

- Modern conveniences that help me relax and unwind

- Material possessions

- Ways in which I've been able to bless others with my material blessings

- My home and property

- Positive things about my neighborhood environment

## 7. Professional

- Favorite employers I had, and why I enjoyed working for them

- Positive things about my job

- Positive things about my coworkers

- Businesses I've owned and operated

- Positive things about past and present employees

- People who helped me advance in my work and career

- People and things that helped me learn the knowledge and skills I need for my work

- People who helped me through difficult times in my work and career

- Fun times I've had at work

- Ways in which my work makes a difference in the lives of others

- Everything my job or career enables me to do and enjoy

- People who taught me a strong work ethic

- Lessons I've learned in working with honesty and integrity

- Times God helped me overcome temptations to steal, cheat, or be dishonest

- Employers, coworkers, and clients who forgave me for mistakes, oversights, and shortcomings

## 8. Financial

- Sources of personal income

- Growth I've helped bring about in my company or organization

- Savings

- Special gifts and blessings

- Successful investments

- Retirement plans

- People who taught me how to manage money

- Lessons I learned about handling money
- Ways in which I've learned to be faithful in that which is least, so the Lord can entrust me with true riches
- Ways in which I've seen blessings through tithing

## 9. Creative

- People who helped me learn music or an instrument
- People who appreciate my creativity
- People who helped me learn art
- People who taught me creative writing, and what I learned
- People who taught me in other creative areas (photography, dance, drama, storytelling, etc.)
- Creative works I've been able to bless others with
- Ways in which God inspired me in my creativity

## 10. Adventure

- Places I've been able to travel
- Things I've learned in my travels
- Outdoor adventures I've enjoyed
- Those who helped me learn the skills I use in my adventures (skiing, biking, backpacking, skydiving, rock climbing, etc.)
- Concerts, performances, and museums I visited
- Things I accomplished outside my comfort zone, and what it did for me

## 11. Legacy

- Virtues I instilled in my children, and ways I see those virtues in their lives
- Values I learned and passed on to others, and how they helped people
- Organizations in which I volunteer my time and effort, and how I can make a difference in people's lives and the organizations

## 12. Character

- Times I realized how the Lord did within me what I could not do for myself

- Times and ways I noticed the Holy Spirit producing fruit of the spirit in my life (love, joy, peace, patience, kindness, goodness, faithfulness, gentleness, and self-control)

- Times the Lord helped me do the right thing, even when no one was looking

- People who taught and inspired me to develop character

- Times I stuck to my word, even when it was difficult

- Trials, tribulations, and temptations in which the Lord has strengthened me

## 13. Community and Nation

- The president and vice president and their families

- Cabinet members

- Supreme Court justices and other federal justices

- My senators and representatives

- My governor and state cabinet members

- My state senators and legislators

- My state Supreme Court and other state justices

- My local government officials

- My local school board members, schools, teachers, staff, and students

- Local law enforcement and first responders

## 14. Worldwide

- My brothers and sisters in Christ who are being persecuted for their faith

- Persecutors whom Christ is turning toward Him

- Everywhere God's Word is available throughout the earth, whether written or spoken

- Freedom for victims of human trafficking

- Missions and missionaries

- Charitable organizations

- Freedom and prosperity for the oppressed

- God's blessings and miracles being proclaimed boldly

## Other Gratitude Prompts

- 
- 
- 
- 
-

# THE SCIENCE OF GRATITUDE

Scientists are finally discovering the benefits of what God has been telling us to do for millennia—give thanks. I happened upon the research being conducted on gratitude quite by accident. I now realize my findings were by divine appointment, and have dramatically changed my life for the better. May your life also be transformed as you discover the amazing benefits of keeping a gratitude journal.

I've believed in practicing gratitude daily for many years. At the beginning of my prayer journal, I had a note: "Today I am thankful for…" I would read that each morning and thank God for His blessings. Yet I ended up thanking Him for the same things each morning.

I read about the power of gratitude in Dr. Daniel Amen's book *Change Your Brain, Change Your Life*.[1] He performed separate brain scans while patients focused on what they were grateful for and what worried them. The thankful scans revealed a much healthier brain than those taken of fearful, worried minds. Dr. Amen now encourages his readers to *write down* five things they are grateful for each day. This practice not only makes people happier; it improves the health of their brain.

I followed his advice and wrote down what I was thankful for instead of just thinking of my blessings. My thanksgiving was more detailed and varied, and my overall mood improved.

In his book *Gratitude Works![2]* Dr. Robert Emmons explains how years of research have yielded the following results with people who keep a gratitude journal:

- Higher levels of positive emotions such as joy, enthusiasm, love, happiness, and optimism

- Protection from the destructive impulses of envy, resentment, greed, and bitterness

- Coping more effectively with everyday stress

- Increased resilience in the face of trauma-induced stress

- Recover more quickly from illness

- Enjoy more robust physical health

- Sleep one-half hour more per evening

- Exercise 33 percent more each week compared to persons who are not keeping gratitude journals

- Hypertensives can achieve a 10 percent reduction in systolic blood pressure and decrease their dietary fat intake by up to 20 percent

- Increased feelings of connectedness, improved relationships, and even altruism

- Feel more loving, more forgiving, and closer to God

- Increased feelings of energy, alertness, enthusiasm, and vigor

- Success in achieving personal goals

- Better coping with stress

- A sense of closure in traumatic memories

- Bolstered feelings of self-worth and self-confidence

- Solidified and secure social relationships

- Generosity and helpfulness

- Prolonging of the enjoyment produced by pleasurable experiences

- Improved cardiac health

- A greater sense of purpose and resilience

A series of studies[3] found that gratitude journaling also helped heart failure patients. Practicing gratitude reduced their inflammation and cardiac risk.

Scientific studies have proven the manifold benefits to us when we obey God's command to give thanks.

# NOTES

1. Daniel G. Amen, *Change Your Brain, Change Your Life*, revised Kindle edition, (New York: Harmony Books, 2015), 120–22.

2. Robert A. Emmons, *Gratitude Works! A 21-Day Program for Creating Emotional Prosperity*, Wiley Online Library, Kindle edition, 344–60.

3. Paul J. Mills and Laura Redwine, "Can Gratitude Be Good for Your Heart?" *Greater Good Magazine,* October 25, 2017, Greater Good Science Center, UC Berkeley, https://greatergood.berkeley.edu/article/item/ can_gratitude_be_good_for_your_heart.

## ABOUT THE AUTHOR

Judy Ransom's passion for communicating biblical truths led her to speak and teach at Bible conferences, retreats, and churches for over forty years. She's developed practical tools and literature to help Christians live victorious lives.

The recipient of two *Living Water* awards, Judy's work is published in *The Upper Room* and *Emerald Coast Review.* She writes for *GO! Christian Magazine* and is a copy editor for the publication.

Judy lives in Northwest Florida with her husband, Steve. Parents of three adult children, they've owned and operated a small business since 1986.

A member of Word Weavers and Christians United for Israel, Judy's love for education supports at-risk youth in a school mentor program where she volunteers her marketing, communications, and graphic design skills. Judy loves hiking, music, and healthy cooking.

### FREE GIFT!

Visit **judyransom.com** for a *free study guide* to *The Secret to Health and Happiness.* This guide will help you develop deeper gratitude, more forgiveness, and a closer relationship with God. Designed for individual study or a twelve-week small group Bible study.

Made in the USA
Monee, IL
08 November 2020